Garden Way's Guide to

Food Drying

by
Phyllis Hobson

Illustrations by Wendy Edelson

Garden Way 🌼 *Publishing*
Charlotte, Vermont 05445

Library of Congress Cataloging in Publication Data

   Hobson, Phyllis.
     Garden Way's guide to food drying.

   Includes index.
    1. Food—Drying.   2. Cookery (Dried foods)
3. Menus. I. Title.
TX609.H59   641.4'4   79-27726
ISBN 0-88266-155-8

Contents

Introduction

Who invented drying foods? We like to think some prehistoric hunter and his mate discarded a chunk of meat beside their cave fire, and a few days later noticed it had turned black and dry. Curious and daring, one of them chewed into it, uttered the Cro-Magnon equivalent of "Not bad," and slowly realized that here was a way to save food for the leaner days that came so regularly.

By the time records were being kept, the drying of food was widespread. Phoenicians and other fishermen were drying their catches in the open air. The Chinese were sun-drying leaves of their tea.

In this country Indians taught early settlers how to dry corn and grind it into meal. Jerky was made from the meat of bear, deer, elk, and buffalo found in the forests and on the plains of this country. The French had invented a dehydrator to dry vegetables by 1795, while American families were still using fire, sun, and smoke to dry their grapes, herbs, peppers, and meats.

Today a desire for natural, healthful, and inexpensive methods of food preservation has put dehydration in modern kitchens. People in all walks of life can dry many kinds of food in all kinds of weather at home.

The art of drying foods is a natural alternative to canning and freezing and benefits the family on a tight budget, because drying fruits, vegetables, grains, and breakfast cereals can offer a low-cost, energy-efficient way of eating for less. Drying foods benefits the hiker, the camper, the skier or the fisherman looking for a compact food supply light enough to carry in a knapsack. It benefits the housewife looking for delicious, healthful snacks to offer her family, and it benefits vacationers with two homes, because drying can be a safe way to store food over the winter. Drying is an ideal way of storing foods for those who live in isolated locations where electricity to operate a freezer may be undependable or non-existent, and it is a good way to stockpile an emergency supply in a small storage area.

The goal of drying foods is to remove excess moisture, getting the water content down to 5 percent to 25 percent, so bacteria which cause decay cannot survive. Since dried foods are only one-half to one-twelfth the weight and bulk of the original food, a small, dry, cool closet will provide all the storage space needed for a winter's supply of food. If dried food is protected by airtight packaging, it will keep indefinitely.

Compared with canning, drying foods is simplicity itself. There are no complicated procedures to learn or potentially dangerous pieces of equipment to operate. You don't need a pressure canner or a hot water bath canner, nor will you have to shop for glass canning jars and boxes of canning lids. Neither will you have to have jar lifters, filling funnels, and tongs. The only special equipment manufactured for drying is a dehydrator, and it is possible to dry without one. Everything else, from oven drying trays to storage jars, you already have on hand or you can make from castoffs.

Compared with freezing, drying is inexpensive and worry-free. Even at today's increased electric rates, it costs approximately twenty-five to fifty cents to dry a dehydrator full of food. Drying in the sun or with an oven pilot flame is absolutely free. It costs from $5 to $20 per month to operate a food freezer, depending on the efficiency of the freezer, the amount of food it contains and the electricity rate in your area.

Even if drying food were not simpler, less expensive and more convenient, many people might still prefer dried foods for their taste. Dried apricots, dried apple slices and raisins compare well with fresh fruits, and honey-dipped pineapple slices, chewy, fruity leathers, and tough, tangy meat jerky have a universal appeal.

Because drying is a more natural method of preservation than canning and freezing, many people believe drying foods preserves more of the nutritional values present in raw foods, and a USDA study backs up this belief. Vitamins are lost in blanching, a pretreatment necessary for some vegetables before drying, but this nutritional loss can be kept to a minimum if the foods are steam blanched for no more than the specified time.

Almost any food can be dried by following the instructions in this book, which are aimed at preserving as much of the nutrients and the flavor of the food as possible.

Will your dried food be as good as what you can buy on the market? Commerical manufacturers have the advantage of expensive freeze-drying equipment, but you have the advantage of sweet, tree-ripened fruit and just-picked, garden-fresh vegetables. Your own homegrown fruits and vegetables, the raw products from which your dried foods are made, should be more delicious and nutritious than those the food processors have, so yours should be better than theirs.

Drying Foods Can Save You Money

If you're having trouble keeping up with the ever-increasing cost of food, a selection of dried foods on your pantry shelf can save your food budget as much as $1,000 a year.

You can save the most money, of course, by drying fruits and vegetables from your own garden or foods that otherwise would go to waste. Drying is not only a safe, easy way of preserving your excess garden harvest; it also is an inexpensive method. Drying costs less than canning and freezing in equipment, energy and storage space.

Even if you don't plant a garden, you can still save money by drying foods at home. During the harvest season fruits and vegetables can be purchased cheaply by the bushel at the country markets and roadside stands.

1

Watch also for specials at the produce department of your favorite supermarket. Bananas flecked with brown which often sell for half-price make excellent fruit leathers. Mushrooms and vegetables often are marked down because a new shipment is due.

Drying also can be a way of saving money by avoiding waste. When you have leftover cooked meat or cooked vegetables, they can be chopped fine and dried, then enjoyed another time months later. Leftover vegetable soup, for instance, can be pureed in the blender, dried on sheets of plastic wrap and eaten as a leather.

Save money too by drying processed grain products. Ready-to-eat purchased breakfast cereals, noodles, and croutons are expensive not because of their ingredients, but because of the time involved in their preparation. Sometime when you have more time than money, you can make them ahead, and dry them for busy days.

If there is a baby at your house, you can save money usually spent on commercially canned baby foods by cooking your own fresh fruits and vegetables just until tender, then straining them with the help of a food mill or Squeezo Strainer. Dry the puree according to the directions for Dried Tomato Puree; then package in small, one-serving packages. To prepare baby's meal, add warm water to the powder until the mixture is the consistency you prefer.

At birthday and Christmas time, or any time a gift is in order, save money with a very special gift:

● For your sweet-toothed friends, save your prettiest peanut butter, pickle or jelly jars, paint the lids, decorate with ribbon bow and fill with a mixture of dried fruits made according to the directions under Drying Fruits.

● For your nature-loving friends, package an assortment of dried soups and stews for their next camping trip. Directions are in the next section, Drying Foods for Hiking and Camping.

● For your young (and young at heart) friends, package a mixed variety of fruit leather strips in plastic wrap and tie with a big ribbon. You'll find the directions under Leathers.

● For your elegant friends, package several different aromatic sachets in colorful nylon nets. Tie with a matching ribbon and attach a list of the ingredients. Several recipes for sachets and potpourries are in the chapter, Drying Flower Petals.

● And for your gourmet friends, fill small baby food jars with dried herbs and herb mixtures (See the Drying Herbs chapter). Paste pretty labels on the jars and include a few recipes on decorative file cards.

Drying Foods For Hiking and Camping

Almost every well-stocked sporting goods store has a display of packaged, dehydrated foods developed especially for the hunter, the camper and the back-packing hiker. It's an appetizing array: vegetable-beef stew, chicken noodle soup, peach cobbler, scrambled eggs and bacon, and potato soup. These meal-size packages are convenient for camping trips where there is no refrigeration, and keeping fresh foods is a problem. They are small enough for canoeing trips where there is little space for supplies and light enough in weight for backpacking.

But those convenient little packages are expensive. A package containing the ingredients for a main dish of beef and noodles or vegetable-beef stew to serve four persons costs $5 to $6. A scrambled egg breakfast with biscuits costs $4 to $5 for four people. At these prices, a weekend supply of dried foods for a camping trip for a family of four could cost $50 to $60.

But the same supply of camping foods can be dried and packaged at home for $10 or less. If the fruits and vegetables are harvested from your garden, the cost may be almost nothing.

Some of the dried foods that would fit well in a backpack for hiking trips where cooking facilities are not available are:

Beef, venison and hamburger jerky, granola cereal, crackers, instant soups (powdered dried green peas, tomatoes or asparagus), any dried fruits, fruit and vegetable leathers, and any dried vegetables you enjoy eating in the dried state, such as zucchini, parsnips and sprouts.

For camping trips, where dried foods may be cooked over a campfire or a commercial camping stove, a complete menu of nourishing meals can be created from a supply of home-dried foods supplemented by a few staples from your grocer's shelves.

The following sample menu for a weekend camping trip can be made using foods dried at home:

Saturday Breakfast:
    Rehydrated apricot halves
      or slices
    Scrambled eggs
    Whole grain biscuits
    Hot chocolate

Saturday Lunch:
    Chicken-noodle soup
    Cheese-topped crackers
    Milk
    Whole grain cookies

Saturday Dinner:
    Hot tomato broth
    Campfire stew
    Blueberry biscuits
    Banana chip pudding
    Milk
    Herb tea

Sunday Breakfast:
    Tomato juice
    Whole grain pancakes
    Milk

Sunday Dinner:
    Beef and potatoes cooked in
      foil
    Green beans and tomatoes
    Cherry cobbler
    Milk
    Herb tea

Sunday Supper:
    Campfire beans and ham
    Cornbread
    Cooked apples
    Milk
    Herb tea

If you wish to use this menu to feed two adults and two children for a weekend, you'll need the following home-dried foods. Recipes follow.

Chicken-Noodle Soup Mix
Campfire Stew Mix
Beef and Potatoes in Foil
Campfire Beans and Ham
Scrambled Egg Mix
½ cup dried cheese
½ cup dried egg powder
1 cup dried apple slices
1¼ cups dried apricot halves or slices
½ cup dried banana chips
¼ cup dried blueberries
1 cup dried cherries
¼ cup dried plums
12 cups Whole Grain Mix
Crackers (see "Drying Grain Products")

1 cup dried green beans
½ cup dried tomatoes
¾ cup dried tomato powder
Herb tea mixture

Other foods needed:
Butter or margarine
Pancake syrup
Salt and pepper
Instant coffee
Instant cocoa mix
1 large box powdered milk
⅔ cup brown sugar
1 cup granulated sugar
1 package vanilla flavored instant pudding

RECIPES FOR CAMPING DISHES

CHICKEN-NOODLE SOUP MIX

½ cup dried chicken cubes
½ cup dried noodles
¼ cup chopped dried carrots
¼ cup chopped dried celery

¼ cup dried green peas
1 tablespoon chopped dried onion
2 tablespoons chicken bouillon powder or 6 chicken bouillon cubes

Combine all ingredients and mix well. Seal in a plastic freezer bag. To serve, simmer over a campfire or camp stove in 2 quarts boiling water until vegetables and meat are tender, about 1 hour. Stir occasionally and add water as necessary. Season to taste with salt and pepper. Serves 4.

REHYDRATING DRIED FRUITS

To prepare dried fruits for camp meals, place 1 cup dried fruit in a quart glass jar or plastic container. Cover with hot or cold water, shake a little and cap with a lid. Let sit in hot sun 4 to 6 hours or soak overnight. Serve without cooking or simmer 5 to 10 minutes over a campfire.

SCRAMBLED EGG MIX

1 cup dried egg powder (see "Drying Dairy Products")
¼ cup dry milk powder
¼ cup imitation bacon bits (made of soybeans)

1 tablespoon finely chopped dried onion
1 tablespoon finely chopped dried green pepper

Combine all ingredients and store in a plastic freezer bag. To serve, blend with ½ cup water. Let set 10 minutes. Beat with a fork and cook over hot coals in a skillet in which 1 tablespoon butter or margarine has been melted. Serves 4.

CHEESE TOPPED
CRACKERS

Combine ¼ cup dried cheese with ¼ cup softened butter or margarine. Spread over homemade crackers (see "Drying Grain Products"). Heat in Dutch oven or reflector oven.

HOT TOMATO
BROTH

Place 3 tablespoons powdered tomato puree in a cup. Fill cup with boiling water and stir well. Season to taste with salt. Serve hot or cold.

CAMPFIRE STEW

1 cup dried beef cubes
½ cup dried potato slices
½ cup dried carrot slices
½ cup dried onion slices

1 tablespoon beef broth powder or 3
  beef bouillon cubes
2 tablespoons flour
Salt and pepper

Combine all ingredients and store in a plastic freezer bag. To serve, add 2 quarts water in a stewing kettle. Simmer over hot coals or on a camp stove over low heat 1 to 1½ hours, until dried foods are tender. season to taste with salt and pepper.

BANANA CHIP PUDDING

1 package vanilla flavored instant
  pudding

½ cup dried banana chips
½ cup dried milk powder

Mix ingredients well. Store in a plastic freezer bag. To serve, stir in water according to directions on pudding package. Beat with a fork. Divide into 4 dishes. Let set 10 minutes.

BEEF AND POTATOES IN FOIL

2 cups dried beef cubes
2 cups dried potato slices
½ cup dried peas
1 tablespoon dried onion

1 tablespoon beef broth powder
⅛ teaspoon dried garlic
4 pieces heavy duty aluminum foil
Salt and pepper

Mix all ingredients well. Divide onto the 4 pieces of foil. Seal foil squares, using drugstore wrap folds. To serve, open each foil package just enough to add 1 cup water to each. Season to taste with salt and pepper and reseal tightly. Cook over hot coals or in a camp oven 1 to 2 hours. Serve in the foil packages.

GREEN BEANS AND TOMATOES

1½ cups dried green beans
½ cup dried tomatoes, chopped
1 teaspoon dried onion

¼ teaspoon salt
¼ cup dried cheese
4 pieces heavy duty aluminum foil

Mix all ingredients except foil. Divide onto 4 pieces of foil and seal into 4 packages. To serve, open packages enough to add ½ cup water to each. Reseal. Cook over hot coals or in a camp oven 30 to 45 minutes. Serve in foil package.

CAMPFIRE BEANS AND HAM

1½ cups dried beans (Great North-
ern, navy, pinto, etc.)
½ cup dried ham, chopped
¼ cup dried onion, chopped
¼ cup dried carrot, grated

2 tablespoons dried green pepper
1 tablespoon chicken broth powder
or 3 chicken bouillon cubes
1 teaspoon salt
⅛ teaspoon pepper

Mix all ingredients well. Store in a plastic freezer bag. To serve, add to 3 quarts water in a stewing kettle. Simmer over hot coals or medium heat on a camp stove 2 to 3 hours, until beans are tender, stirring occasionally and adding water if necessary.

WHOLE GRAIN BAKING MIX

3 cups whole wheat flour
3 cups unbleached white flour
1 cup wheat germ
4 cups old-fashioned rolled oats
2 cups dried milk powder

4 tablespoons baking powder
1 tablespoon salt
1½ pounds margarine or solid shortening

Combine dry ingredients. Using a pastry blender or electric mixer, cut in margarine to the consistency of fine meal. Spread over dehydrator trays covered with plastic wrap and dry 2 hours at lowest heat setting. Cool, then divide into 8 plastic freezer bags and seal.

Because of the margarine or shortening, this mix will turn rancid in long-term storage at room temperature. It may be stored in the freezer or it will keep well unrefrigerated for a camping trip of a week or more. For longer storage without refrigeration, omit the margarine or shortening and add ¼ cup shortening to each cup dry mix just before using.

To Use Whole Grain Baking Mix: Here are some recipes for using that baking mix.

BISCUITS

To 2 cups whole grain mix add just enough water to make a stiff dough. Divide into 8 pieces and roll each into a ball, then flatten slightly. Place on a piece of ungreased aluminum foil and bake over hot coals or camp stove in a Dutch oven or reflector oven until done through, 15 to 30 minutes, depending on the temperature of the fire. Biscuits may not brown, but should be done through.

BLUEBERRY BISCUITS

Stir in ¼ cup dried blueberries to dry mix before adding water. Proceed as directed above.

WHOLE GRAIN PANCAKES

1 tablespoon dried powdered egg (or 1 egg)
1 tablespoon sugar

3 cups whole grain mix
1 cup water

Combine all ingredients. Stir until dry ingredients are moistened. Add water, if needed, to make a thin batter. Drop by spoonfuls on a hot, greased griddle. Turn once to brown on both sides. Serve immediately with butter or margarine and syrup.

9

WHOLE GRAIN COOKIES

1 tablespoon powdered dried egg (or
   1 egg)
2 cups whole grain mix
⅔ cup brown sugar

⅓ cup water
¼ cup chopped dried plums
¼ cup chopped dried apricots

Blend all ingredients well. Drop by spoonfuls on a greased doubled sheet of aluminum foil, spreading slightly with the back of the spoon. Bake in a stove-top oven or reflector oven over hot coals 10 to 20 minutes. Makes 2 dozen cookies.

WHOLE GRAIN CORNBREAD

1½ cups whole grain mix
¾ cup ground dried corn

1 tablespoon powdered dried egg (or
   1 egg)
½ cup water (about)

Combine all ingredients. Stir just until blended. Pour into a well-greased 8-inch square baking pan or a pan made by folding a doubled thickness of heavy duty aluminum foil into a pan shape, then greasing well. Bake in a camp stove oven or over medium heat or in a Dutch oven or reflector oven over hot coals. Bake until a straw inserted in the middle comes out clean. Baking time depends on the temperature of the fire.

CHERRY CRISP

1 cup dried cherries
½ cup sugar
1½ cups water

2 tablespoons butter or margarine
2 cups whole grain mix
½ cup water

Combine first 4 ingredients and cook over campfire 30 minutes in an iron skillet or Dutch oven. Meanwhile, mix the 2 remaining ingredients in a bowl. Spread over top of hot cherry mixture. Bake in reflector oven or camp stove oven 20 to 30 minutes or cover Dutch oven with a lid and cook 20 to 30 minutes over hot coals.

Recipes for other dried foods suitable for outdoor cooking can be found under "Dried Soup Mixtures."

10

Dried Food Snacks

Dried foods make delicious, nutritious snacks, either eaten as is, combined with other dried foods, or when used to make baked and unbaked treats.

For children, dried food snacks can be a healthful substitute for candy or empty-calorie cookies. Remember, however, that dried foods—especially fruits—are highly concentrated foods, so smaller amounts should be eaten.

DRIED FRUITS

For "walking around" snacks for children, dried fruits are ideal. Dried apple slices, banana chips, dried apricots, and plums are favorites.

For dried fruit mixtures, fruits should be chopped and dried separately, then combined. Seal dried fruits and dried fruit combinations in small packages for children. For adults, serve in a covered candy dish.

Some good dried fruit combinations are:

- Sliced strawberries, bananas, and pineapple
- Chopped apricots and bananas
- Chopped apples, cherries, and coconut
- Sliced peaches, orange peel, and bananas
- Chopped plums, bananas, and nuts

DRIED VEGETABLES

Some dried vegetables also may be eaten "as is." Many people like to snack on dried cucumber, parsnips, and zucchini slices.

Crisp dried sprouts are great for snacking and may be eaten alone or in combination with nuts, raisins or dried, chopped apples.

Many of the recipes in this book make excellent snacks. Some of the good, whole-grain foods include granola, crackers, and corn crisps. All are included in the "Drying Grain Products" section.

For foods rich in protein, try beef, venison, or hamburger jerky in the "Meats" section. For a liquid snack, add boiling water or boiling hot beef broth to dried, powdered tomato puree. And for a snack that has been a favorite of both children and adults for generations, nothing can beat the fruit and vegetable leathers.

The following are additional recipes for snacks using dried foods.

DRIED APPLE BREAD

1 cup dried apples	¼ teaspoon cloves
1 cup water	2 cups all-purpose flour
2 teaspoons soda	¼ teaspoon salt
½ cup shortening	¾ cup chopped dried plums
1 cup sugar	¼ cup dried seedless grapes
1 egg	1 cup walnuts, chopped
1 teaspoon cinnamon	

Combine apples and water in a blender. Add soda. In a large mixing bowl, cream shortening and sugar. Add egg and mix well. In another bowl, mix other dry ingredients and add to creamed mixture alternately with applesauce. Stir in dried plums, grapes, and nuts. Pour into greased 9 × 12-inch loaf pan. Bake in 350° F. oven 40 to 45 minutes.

PEANUT-BANANA DROPS

3 cups old-fashioned rolled oats
1¼ cups chunk-style peanut butter
1 cup dried banana slices, chopped

½ cup honey
½ cup butter or margarine

Spread oats over a cookie sheet or jelly roll pan in a 250° F. oven. Toast until lightly browned, 15 to 20 minutes, stirring occasionally. Meanwhile, in a heavy skillet, melt peanut butter, honey, and butter or margarine, stirring until smooth. Stir in oats and dried bananas. Drop by rounded spoonfuls onto waxed paper. Chill until firm. Store in refrigerator. Makes 4 dozen snacks.

CARROT-OAT COOKIES

1 cup brown sugar
½ cup shortening
3 eggs
⅔ cup milk
1 cup dried grated carrots
2 cups all-purpose flour
1 teaspoon baking powder
½ teaspoon salt

½ teaspoon baking soda
½ teaspoon cinnamon
1½ cups rolled oats
1½ cups dried seedless grapes or chopped dried plums
½ cup chopped nuts
1 tablespoon dried grated orange peel

Mix together sugar, shortening, eggs, milk, and carrots. Let stand 10 minutes. Meanwhile, combine dry ingredients. Mix with dried fruit, nuts, and dried orange peel. Drop by spoonfuls on greased cookie sheet. Bake 10 to 12 minutes in 350° F. oven. Makes 4 dozen cookies.

DRIED BRAN SNACKS

½ cup chunk-style peanut butter   ½ cup dry milk powder
½ cup honey   3 tablespoons sesame seeds
3 tablespoons butter or margarine   3 tablespoons sunflower seeds
2 cups bran cereal   ¼ cup dried apricots, chopped
½ cup whole wheat flour

Melt peanut butter, honey, and butter or margarine over low heat, stirring well to blend. Add remaining ingredients and stir well. Press firmly in the bottom of a 9 × 12-inch baking pan. Cool and cut into squares. No baking is necessary.

Dehydrator: Spread cut bran squares over bottom of drying trays, removing every other tray. Dry at 110° F. 4 to 6 hours, until crisp and no longer sticky.

Sun: Spread cut squares over drying trays and place in full sun, covering with cheesecloth to protect from insects and birds. Dry 6 to 8 hours, until crisp.

Oven or Homemade Dryer: Place squares without touching over drying trays. Place trays in an oven or homemade dryer preheated to 110° F. Dry 4 to 6 hours.

How to Dry Foods

Just as with freezing and canning, the best quality dried foods must begin with the best quality foods available. Fruit and vegetables to be dried should be picked when they are at their peak of flavor. Most vegetables are best picked while they are still slightly immature. Harvest peas and beans when the pods are still green and succulent. Spinach and other leafy vegetables should be picked before the leaves reach full size. Most root vegetables should be pulled while still undersized. Corn should be picked before the natural sugars turn to starch, while the kernels are succulent enough to squirt out juice when punctured with the thumbnail. Kole vegetables—including broccoli, cabbage and kohlrabi—should be picked after the vegetable is well formed, but before it becomes strong-tasting. Brussels sprouts are best after the first frost.

Fruits, including berries and tomatoes, should be left to ripen thoroughly before picking. Peaches, apricots, and apples are sweeter and more flavorful when tree-ripened.

In general, the faster a food is dried, the better the quality—but temperatures can't be so high that the food is cooked. Drying is speeded and quality improved if the food is as dry as possible when the process begins. Pick fruits, vegetables, and herbs in late morning, when the sun has dried off the early morning dew. Drain cooked vegetables well. Wipe off washed fruit. Do not soak any food for more than five or ten minutes. Most fruits and vegetables should be peeled to permit the air to penetrate the inner pulp.

Drying also is speeded if as much food surface as possible is exposed to the air. To do this, cut food pieces as small—especially as thin—as possible, with a knife, or in a food processor or salad maker. Some vegetables, such as onions, green peppers, and turnips, may be coarsely grated in a blender or shredded with a hand-held grater.

The foods then are ready to be pretreated according to the directions in the chapter, "To Pretreat or Not To Pretreat". Then they may be dried according to one of the three methods which follow.

After drying, foods should be cooled, tested for any sign of moisture (see "Testing and Storing Dried Foods"), then stored and labeled.

Three methods of drying are recommended for each of the foods listed in this book. Each method has its advocates and its advantages. The method you choose will depend upon the climate and the environment in which you live, your finances, and the amount of drying you'll be doing.

The three recommended methods are:

DEHYDRATOR

Drying foods was once a simple procedure. The food was harvested and spread out in the sun to dry. After a few days, it was brought inside and stored for the winter. The results weren't always perfect. Sometimes the food spoiled before it dried. Dried fruits had a tendency to turn brown and hard. Sometimes dried vegetables were tough and stringy. Dried meats resembled well-tanned shoe leather. But once they were refreshed and cooked, sun-dried foods were quite acceptable, especially when good cooks came up with such dishes as Dried Apple Pie and Fruit Cakes.

Times have changed, however, as have our environments. Some of us live in the cities, where there are no expanses of unfiltered sunlight in which to dry foods, where dust and chemicals and other pollutants will contaminate any foods spread out to dry. Some of us live too close to the leaded fumes of highways, to railroad tracks and in the pathways of insecticide sprays. Some of us live in climates too sunless, too humid, or too cold. We cannot depend on the sun to dry our food.

Our tastes have changed. We have become accustomed to snowy white dried apples and bright orange dried apricots. Our palates have been educated. We no longer want our dried foods to taste like dried foods.

And so to accommodate our changed living conditions and our educated palates, a modern kitchen appliance has been designed to dry our food with speed, efficiency, and a minimum of trouble. It's called a dehydrator.

To dry foods in an electric dehydrator, it is only necessary to prepare the food, fill the trays, and turn it on. The best of the dehydrators have thermostatically controlled heat settings and fans which blow the warm air over the foods. A good, well-designed dehydrator is so automatic it is almost impossible to overdry or scorch the food being dried.

Many foods do not even need to be pretreated before drying in a dehydrator, because the forced air dries the surface of the food before it can discolor. Many advocates claim that dehydrator air movement makes any pretreating unnecessary, but our tests show that some forms of pretreatment are required for best results in some foods.

The price of a good dehydrator may vary from $100 to $300, depending on its size, the construction materials, and its design. For those who would dry a large portion of their food supply, an electric dehydrator could be a good investment, roughly equivalent to the cost of a household's supply of canners, canning jars, and other equipment needed for canning.

A dehydrator should be used indoors, in a dry, well-ventilated room. A kitchen is not necessarily the best place, since the humidity often caused by cooking hinders its operation.

To operate an electric dehydrator, just plug it into an 110-volt outlet and preheat to the desired temperature while the food is being prepared for drying. Recommended temperatures are 115° F. for uncooked fruits, 120° F. for vegetables and some cooked fruits, 110° F. for leaf herbs, 140° for meat and 115° F. for grains.

Estimated drying times and exact temperatures are included in the specific drying instructions for each food in the section to follow. All drying times listed for foods are estimates. Exact times will depend on the efficiency of the dehydrator, the humidity of the air in the room and the amount of moisture in the food.

Some form of preparation is needed for most foods. Many must be peeled because the drying air cannot penetrate the skin. Slicing or chopping helps expose more surface to the warm moving air, speeding the drying process and producing better results. Some foods must be blanched or dipped to retard discoloration and enzyme growth which would cause loss of flavor and nutrients. The pretreatment of foods before drying is covered in detail in the chapter "To Pretreat or Not To Pretreat."

To begin the drying process, spread the prepared foods evenly over the dehydrator trays in a thin layer. Different foods may be dried at the same time, but very moist foods should not be dried with almost-dry foods. Foods with very strong odors or flavors should be dried alone. Foods which have been pretreated with sulfur fumes never should be dried in a dehydrator.

Food should be examined and stirred or turned at least once while drying. At the same time, the trays should be rotated, front to back, side to side and top to bottom.

As the drying progresses, the food will shrink and you will be tempted to consolidate trays and add more food to the dehydrator. You may do so, but it will lengthen the drying time to crowd the almost-dry foods on the trays. It is better to wait until the first batch is completely dried before adding more food to the dehydrator.

Dehydrator drying is so trouble-free you can leave the dehydrator operating overnight or while you're away from home. If your days are busy, you can load the dehydrator in the morning before you leave for work and let it run all day with complete safety. If a dryer load is almost dry at bedtime, just turn the heat down to 105° or 110° and go to bed. By morning, the food will be ready to store.

To help you dry foods in a dehydrator, you'll need knives and a strainer or maybe a blender. If you want to make leather, you'll need some plastic wrap or a special leather-making sheet. Dehydrators come complete with their own trays.

SUN

If you are blessed with clean air, low humidity, and an abundance of hot, sunshiny days, sun drying is the least expensive and simplest method of preserving foods.

The advantages to sun drying are obvious. It's absolutely free. It does not require an outlay for electricity. There isn't even an investment in equipment. All the necessary equipment can be made at home.

If you live where sun drying is practical, by all means try it. Even if your location is marginal, you can use the sun when possible, then fall back on a dehydrator or the oven to finish off a batch on those days when a sudden rainstorm or a low cloud ceiling hampers your sun-drying operation.

Because sun drying is slower and the food is exposed for a longer period of time, pretreating is more important than for drying in a dehydrator. Specific instructions are listed in the chapter on pretreating. *Sun drying is the only method recommended for fruits that have been sulfured.*

After pretreating, foods to be sun dried are spread over the drying trays and placed in a well-ventilated place in full sun. Foods that are attractive to birds and insects must be covered with a layer of cheesecloth propped up to keep it from touching the food.

Every few hours during the drying period, the food should be turned or stirred to expose all surfaces to the sun. Take trays inside at night to prevent the foods from reabsorbing moisture from the dew. Any time out of the sun, of course, is "down time" and is not included in the drying time estimates.

All drying times given for sun drying under specific foods are estimates since the time required for any one food will vary, depending on the temperature, the amount of sunshine, the humidity in the air, the amount of air movement and the amount of moisture in the food.

To dry foods in the sun, you'll need a number of drying trays, preparation equipment such as knives, a peeler, a strainer or blender, plastic wrap for making leathers, cheesecloth for covering foods and containers for storage.

Drying trays may be cookie sheets or homemade wooden trays, but drying is speeded if air is allowed to circulate freely around the food, so trays made of fiberglass or stainless steel screening work best. Don't use galvanized screen. It will contaminate the food. And be careful about those wooden trays. The odors of such woods as pine and cedar will transfer to the food being dried on them.

19

Unlike other drying methods, there is no capacity limit in sun drying. The only limit to the amount of food which can be dried at one time is the number of trays available.

Before storing, foods dried in the sun should be placed in an oven set at 125° F. for 30 minutes to kill any insect eggs which may have been deposited on them or they may be stored in glass or metal containers and set in the freezer for a day or two.

OVEN OR
HOMEMADE DRYER

For drying small amounts of food or in an emergency when rain brings the sun drying operation to a halt, an oven may be used for drying foods.

Depending on its design and size, a homemade dryer also may be used for drying foods in large or small batches. Some homemade dryers may do the job almost as well as a commercial dehydrator.

Drying foods in an oven sometimes is better than sun drying, because it is possible to have controlled, even temperatures, but it has the disadvantage of poor air circulation, and air movement is necessary for even drying. Air circulation can be improved by leaving the door ajar a few inches and placing an electric fan in front of the door, positioned so it will blow away the moist air as it accumulates.

Although commercial drying trays are available for use in an oven, homemade trays may be made of wooden frames and fiberglass screening. Tray sizes will depend on the oven size, and must provide for circulation of air. There should be one inch of space on each side, three inches at the top and bottom and two and one-half inches between the trays.

You'll also need a thermometer that registers from 100° to 150° F., preparation tools such as knives, a peeler, a strainer or blender, plastic wrap and storage containers.

To dry foods in an oven or homemade dryer, load the trays sparsely with a thin layer of food on each tray. Different foods may be dried at the same time, but foods with different moisture content or with strong flavors or odors should not be dried together.

Using a large, easily read thermometer on the top shelf, warm the oven or dryer to the specified temperature with the gas pilot flame, one or two 150-watt light bulbs or the heat source of the homemade dryer. Place trays in the warm oven or dryer, leaving the door ajar. Set the electric fan in front of the door, directed so it dispels the moist air. Dry according to directions under each food, stirring or turning the food occasionally and rotating trays top to bottom, front to back and side to side every two or three hours.

Foods dried in an oven or homemade dryer must be watched more carefully than those in the sun or in a commercial dehydrator.

If You're Thinking About Buying a Dehydrator

Like other kitchen appliances, home food dehydrators come in an array of sizes and shapes and colors, with a wide assortment of features. There are small-batch dehydrators styled for the apartment kitchen and floor model dehydrators big enough for the farm garden. The size of the heating element varies from 165 to 1,000 watts or more. Some are vented. Some are not.

But unlike purchasing other kitchen appliances, you may have to make your choice without trying out—or even seeing—the food dehydrators available. Comparison shopping is rarely possible because most dehydrators are sold by mail, not by your hometown appliance dealer. It isn't even possible to depend on the reputation of a manufacturer you know and trust, since the manufacturing of dehydrators is a new field and you may not be familiar with the companies making them.

Before you decide what to buy, write to several manufacturers and find out about the materials, the construction, the dimensions, the size and type of heating elements and fans of several models. Specifically ask for construction details about the two trouble spots in dehydrator design, the door and the trays. You'll get brochures, but some of them contain more adjectives than facts.

Ask for a copy of the guarantee; then, if necessary, ask for an explanation of the wording. Most mail order dehydrators come with a limited one-year warranty against defective parts, but do not promise to pay labor costs.

To help you sort out this maze of sizes and features and guarantees, we did some comparison shopping for you. Over a period of several weeks, we tested six dehydrators from six manufacturers, using a variety of foods under a variety of conditions.

The units were tested under home, not laboratory, conditions, since the home is where you would be using it. A few extra inches in size may seem unimportant in the laboratory, but on a kitchen counter with little workspace to spare, size is critical. The noise level may seem minor in a testing lab, but in a kitchen often the additional noise of the dehydrator fan is more noticeable.

We dried some of the foods normally dried at home; chopped green peppers, diced carrots, sliced apples. Drying times varied from dryer to dryer and from day to day, according to the weather and the amount of moisture in the foods. On the whole, results were better tasting and better looking than foods dried in the sun. Dried green pepper bits were a bright green. Dried carrot slices were bright orange. The taste and aroma of most of the foods dried in the dehydrator were excellent.

Then we gave the dehydrators every impossible task you might—but probably wouldn't—give them in your kitchen. We dried foods that are difficult to dry—whole, plump, green lima beans, tomato quarters, chunks of wet squash. On a soggy, rainy day we dried peach halves and thick banana slices. It took longer and the results were not always as bright-colored as food dried in smaller pieces or in less humid weather, but the results were good.

We deliberately made some mistakes. We overloaded the dehydrators—the foods lost some color and it took longer. We left food in the dryers hours past the dry stage to see if they would overdry. When a batch was not quite ready at bedtime, we left it on overnight. We found that the dehydrators were safe to leave operating overlong and overnight.

We also tried not leaving them on overnight. At bedtime we shut off dehydrators loaded with half-dried foods, then turned them on again in the morning. It took an hour or so for the foods to recover from the moisture acquired during the night, but drying resumed and the results were good.

Sometimes we followed manufacturer's directions exactly. Sometimes we did not. We dried foods at too low and too high temperatures until we found the just-right temperature for the results we wanted. We found the best temperature was not always the one recommended by the manufacturer.

AREAS OF DISAGREEMENT

There were other areas in which we sometimes disagreed with the manufacturer. Most of the instruction sheets and books accompanying the dehydrators emphasized that the rotation of trays is not necessary with their models because of advance design or a special air flow system. We followed their directions with some batches. We ignored them with others. We found that results were better with every model when trays were rotated, front to back, side to side, and top to bottom, at least once during the drying period. In addition, we found that drying was aided by stirring or turning over the pieces of food at least once or twice.

When we began the testing, we had a definite preference for sun drying, since we live in an isolated area where sun drying is practical. But long before the tests were complete, we were convinced that the new dehydrators definitely have a place in modern home preservation just as logical as the electric freezer and the pressure canner.

On a rural homestead, such as ours, where space and traffic pollution are not problems, usually it is convenient and practical to spread green beans out on trays and set them out in the sun. But there also are periods of several rainy days in a row when this isn't possible. There are many foods, such as peaches and bananas and apples, which are markedly superior when dried in a dehydrator. And there are some foods, notably soups and jerky, which might not be possible to dry at all without the new dehydrators.

Once we decided that dehydrators are here to stay, we began to look around for a permanent place in the kitchen to put one. Although most manufacturers say they are working to perfect a compact cabinet with a large capacity, some of the models are too large to keep for long on the kitchen counter. Yet these models must stay on the counter because they are too heavy and bulky for most people to wrestle off and back onto the counter every day or two during the harvest season.

In spite of the convenience of dehydrators and the quality of the food they produce, we found the size of the units, the constant noise of the fans, and humidity they add to the air in an already-humid room a little overpowering in a small kitchen. Most manufacturers' directions specify that they should not be used outdoors, but if you're buying a dehydrator, you might look for a spot on an enclosed back porch, a utility room or even a spare bedroom. We found a small metal utility table on casters ideal for holding a dryer and for moving it from one room to another.

In spite of their differences in design, the models tested had a number of similar problems. Five of the six models had problems with the door. The hinges were flimsy, the door didn't quite fit the opening or didn't latch well. We had difficulty keeping the door of one model from falling off during drying.

Food trays seem to be another engineering problem with dehydrators. In their search for a lightweight, non-toxic material on which to place the food, most manufacturers have settled on some form of plastic in one of two styles. Trays made of plastic screen embedded in a plastic or aluminum frame were included with four of the models. We preferred these one-piece trays but found they must be handled with both hands when loaded with food—a difficult feat when the trays must be juggled in order to open the dryer door.

The two-piece trays included with two of the dehydrators consisted of a square of plastic mesh to be placed on top of a plastic frame. One is to be fastened down, the other is not. These trays were designed for easier cleaning and it's true that the pieces of mesh are easily soaked in the kitchen sink, but we found that liquid from very juicy foods tended to settle in the grooves around the rim of the plastic frame, which was difficult to clean. These trays also were a little harder to handle when loaded.

The six models tested ranged from square and compact to almost too large for the kitchen counter. Doors were hinged on the bottom, on the side, and not at all.

Because our comparisons showed that the size of the dehydrator is not necessarily an indication of its capacity, dehydrator cabinets were measured to indicate needed counter space, not food capacities. Trays were measured not by their overall size, as the manufacturers do, but by their usable, food-holding area.

The dehydrators tested were all electric. There also are a limited number of non-electric dehydrators which fit into the oven of the kitchen range. The advertisements say these dehydrators utilize the pilot flame of a gas range or the oven light of an electric range to dry foods without cost. These were not tested.

BEE BEYER FOOD DRYER

This is one of the best engineered, best performing dehydrators tested. It also is the most expensive. Bee Beyer offers several models: Wood 101, $139.99 to $169.99 (wood exterior); Arrow 2, $199.99 (all metal with polyethylene trays); Arrow 1, $239.99 (all metal with stainless steel trays). Only the highest priced model was tested.

This model operates on 850 watts, 120 volts and features a high velocity air flow designed to increase the air circulation for high moisture foods. In every test it did just that. Tested at the same time, with the same foods and under identical humidity conditions with each of the other dehydrators, this unit produced excellent results in a shorter time. One of the reasons was the air vent design which allowed for the escape of the moist air on one side while it pulled in dry air from the other. Only one other model tested had separate vents for air intake and escape. Most of the units had no venting systems, but relied on the escape of moist air around loosely fitting doors.

The model tested was larger than some, 12 inches high by 23½ inches wide and 16 inches deep, but it fit on the kitchen counter well. Its baked enamel metal cabinet and smoke Plexiglas door coordinated well with other appliances. The sturdy all-metal construction probably would be longer lasting than some of the mostly-plastic models tested.

The side-hinged door was well constructed, with a metal frame. The latch was not as secure as the Equi-Flow or Harvest Maid models, but unlike any of the other dryers, the door was insulated against heat loss with foam strips at top and bottom. It was a well-constructed door without the usual problems of the side hinge. The trays slid in and out quite well with the door opened at a 90° angle. As a result, the unit required less than thirty inches of counter space.

There were eight sturdy trays with a food-holding surface of 13½ by 15½ inches. The trays were one piece, with polyethylene screen attached to metal frames. Fully loaded, the unit had a potential of almost 12 square feet of drying space.

But there were problems. The trays were well spaced, one inch apart, but they fit the shelves so loosely that the trays caught when sliding in and out, sometimes causing spillage when the trays were full.

We experienced more case hardening—a hazard peculiar to dehydrators—with this dehydrator than with any of the others. Case hardening occurs when the exterior of a piece of food becomes so hard that the interior can't dry. Two batches of celery and potatoes became so hard on the outside that they failed to dry on the inside and subsequently developed mold in storage. However, we were able to dry most fruits and

Bee Beyer Food Dryer.

vegetables at a lower temperature in the Bee Beyer than in the other dryers and most foods dried well in less time.

In all, we liked the looks, the convenience, and the performance of this model. The front featured a clearly marked thermostat control that indicated the temperature every five degrees from 100° to 140° F. In addition, there was a control setting to adjust one of the side vents for air flow control.

Although its price may place it in a different category than other dehydrators tested, the Bee Beyer gave excellent results in dry weather and better than average results in humid and rainy weather. It is manufactured and sold by Bee Beyer, 1154 Roberto Lane, Los Angeles, CA, 90024, and has a limited one-year warranty.

EQUIFLOW FOOD DEHYDRATOR

Equiflow Food Dehydrators are manufactured by B & J Industries, 514 State St., Marysville, Wash., 98270. They also make the lower cost Garden Way 10 Tray Food Dehydrator available from Garden Way Catalog, Charlotte, VT 05445.

Three models are produced—a compact, five-tray dehydrator with five square feet of drying area for $109.95, a ten-tray model with

27

*Equiflow Food
Dehydrator.*

fourteen square feet of drying area for $169.95 and a twenty-tray floor
model with forty-one square feet of drying area for $329.95.

We tested the middle-priced, ten-tray model. This was the most
compact of the dehydrators tested and we found the results well above
average. The cabinet was 15 inches tall, 15 inches wide and 18 inches
deep and was covered with wood-grained plastic laminate. The design
was attractive, uncomplicated, and would coordinate well with almost
any kitchen decor.

The mechanism was as uncomplicated as the cabinet design. A large,
rear-mounted fan blew warm air horizontally across the food trays and
out the top of the door which was slightly ajar on the front.

We especially appreciated the door of this dehydrator. The door, like
the dehydrator itself, was simple, but functional. It was a sheet of
Plexiglas hinged at the bottom for easy opening and easy access to the
trays inside. It was a sturdy door, well hinged, and it latched firmly
without fuss. It is also worth noting that if it should ever be broken, the
door could be replaced easily with another piece of Plexiglas.

The unit had ten 12 × 12-inch trays. We found that a great deal of food
could be dried quickly on this ten square feet of drying area because of
the better-than-average spacing between trays, which were one inch
apart. However, we found we could get better results faster by using five
trays at a time and spacing them farther apart.

This dehydrator performed well in all tests. It had a quiet-running,
eight-inch fan and a 1,000 watt, 120 volt heating element. The model
tested took about ten minutes to reach the desired temperature when
empty.

It was one of the most even-drying of the dehydrators tested and successfully dried batches of shell beans, corn, carrot and celery slices, parsley, and apples very evenly, although the weather was extremely humid. Like most of the dehydrators tested, though, in wet weather it performed not as well on the juicy fruits, such as peaches and tomato slices, on a medium-high setting.

The location and design of the heat selection dial were a little inconvenient. The dial located at the rear right side and had only three settings—"On," "Medium" and "High." There was no Off/On switch. According to the instruction booklet, "Low" ("On" to "Medium") was 90° to 110° F, "Medium" was 115° to 130° F. and "High" was 145° F.

This was an excellent dehydrator and one of the best of those tested, but it would be easier to operate with accuracy if the dial were brought up front and labeled with exact temperatures.

The unit is backed by a one-year warranty and is sold by direct mail from the manufacturer or through the Garden Way Catalog, Charlotte, VT 05445, which also offers a knocked-down version of the mid-priced model.

HARVEST MILLS

The six well-spaced trays of the Little Harvey dehydrator were 14 inches by 15½ inches and not as shallow as most dehydrator trays. We found them deep enough to hold any foods without danger of spilling over while loading into the dryer. There were 1⅜-inch spacings between trays.

Although the food-holding area of the trays measured just over nine square feet, we found that the better spacing of trays allowed us to dry a larger quantity of foods in this model than in the models with nine or ten trays more closely spaced. Carrots and apples retained their bright color and flavor with no pretreatment when slices were dried in just six hours. The trays fit snugly and slid in and out much more easily than in other dehydrators.

The unit was attractive, with minimum use of plastic. The double-walled steel cabinet was painted in a choice of three colors and featured a metal-framed, smoked glass door, the only use of real glass we found. The door was hinged at the bottom, which is convenient for loading and unloading, but the door of the model tested was crooked and did not fit squarely.

This was the largest of the dehydrators tested. It measured 13 inches high by 17 inches wide by 24 inches deep—a bit large for the average kitchen counter, yet too cumbersome to be shifted from place to place.

We found it especially inconvenient to find that the Off/On switch and the temperature dial were in the back, behind the dehydrator, under the kitchen cabinets and completely inaccessible. We could have groped to the back and flicked on the switch, but in order to see to set the temperature dial, it was necessary to pull the unit out from the wall and set the dial with one hand while balancing the dehydrator with the other.

The temperature dial had three settings—95°, 125° and 155°. We found that at 125° this dehydrator performed beautifully. Even in rainy weather the carrot slices dried in it were bright orange and just-right leathery. The zucchini slices were crisp in six hours.

The unit had a 1,000 watt, 120-volt, back-mounted heating element and a six-inch fan. Manufactured by Ideal Harvest, P.O. Box 15481, Salt Lake City, UT 84115, it is sold by direct mail from the factory or through J.C. Penney Co. Suggested retail price is $169.95 for this Little Harvey 100.

Ideal Harvest also manufactures the Sunshine Valley dehydrator, at $89.95. Sunshine Valley is a smaller (13½ inches wide by 13½ inches high by 13 inches deep), lightweight, less expensive model with a 500-watt heating element and a six-inch fan.

Little Harvey.

*Harvest Maid
Dehydrator.*

HARVEST MAID DEHYDRATOR

The Harvest Maid Dehydrator was a good-looking, well designed appliance with a wood-grained vinyl exterior and a solid state circuitry designed to lower operating cost. It operated on 600 watts, 110 volts.

An adjustment vent on the back of the unit allowed the horizontal air flow to be recirculated to reduce energy consumption. A polyurethane foam filter was furnished to cover the rear intake vent to prevent dust from settling on drying foods or handicrafts.

A color-coded temperature selector level plus an Off/On switch were situated conveniently on the front panel beside the door. The door fit well and was hinged on the left, which could be a convenient feature except that the door had to be opened all the way back in order to slide the trays in and out. This not only required a certain amount of caution when handling trays loaded with food, it also required double the amount of counter space—almost forty inches.

The attractive metal cabinet was 21 inches wide by 10 inches tall by 17 inches deep with eight 15-inch square trays spaced one-half inch apart. The trays were two-piece—sheets of plastic mesh fitted onto plastic frames—and designed to simplify cleaning and the removal of sticky foods.

The mesh was designed to be removed from the tray, flexed to flip off the dried-on food, then folded to form a pouring spout to transfer the dried food into containers. The trays could be soaked for easier cleaning and a variety of mesh sizes were available at extra cost.

31

A neat, compact unit, the Harvest Maid tested had a very quiet fan. Excellent results were obtained with a variety of foods dried in it.

Alternative Pioneering Systems, 109 Portland Ave., South, Minneapolis, MN 55401, manufactures two models. FD200 is sold through Sears, Roebuck and Montgomery Ward catalogs for $119.99. Model FD300, the unit tested, is available by direct mail from the manufacturer for $189.95.

EXCALIBUR DEHYDRATOR

A good-sized dehydrator with a painted metal cabinet, the Excalibur featured a left-to-right air flow. The heating element and fan operated on 1,000 watts, 110 volts. Especially helpful were a right-up-front, well numbered temperature dial and a helpful drying guide on the model tested.

We found the two-piece plastic trays sturdier and easier to handle than some others, perhaps because of their smaller size. They were fourteen inches square. The trays were designed for ease of cleaning, with lift-off plastic mesh which set on plastic frames. The trays were spaced 3/4 inch apart in the cabinet.

The overall size of the Excalibur tested was 22 inches wide by 12 inches high by 17 inches deep. There were nine trays with a total of more than twelve square feet of drying area.

The door was not hinged, but set in a groove in the acrylic frame of the cabinet. When it was cool, the door set loosely in the groove, but when the acrylic was heated up in operation, it no longer fit the groove and the door on the model tested fell off several times during operation.

Excalibur Dehydrator.

A wide variety of foods was dried in the Excalibur with satisfactory results, although more time was required than with some models.

A new model, which was not tested, features a 1,100-watt heating element and a ten-inch fan.

The dehydrator tested is priced at $149 and may be purchased by mail from the manufacturer, Excalibur Products, 6083 Power Inn Road, Sacramento, CA 95824, and through other national outlets including the Garden Way Catalog, Charlotte, VT 05445.

*Jack's Food
Dehydrator.*

JACK'S FOOD DEHYDRATOR

This was a small, low-cost unit which was received unassembled. The textured aluminum cabinet was assembled easily in approximately twenty minutes.

Assembled, the cabinet measured 12 inches wide by 16 inches high by 12 inches deep. It had four 11 × 12-inch drawers instead of trays. There was no door. The cabinet was unlined, with a 165-watt heating coil on the bottom of the cabinet. There was no fan and no thermostat.

During preliminary heating tests, the metal cabinet became very hot and heating was uneven. Within thirty minutes, the bottom drawer reached 165°, the second drawer 140°, and the third drawer 110° and the top drawer 80°. During drying, the bottom drawer became too hot to handle and the food on it scorched and had to be discarded.

Unlike directions for other dehydrators, the directions for using this unit suggested the drawers should be switched occasionally. Although we switched drawers every hour, the food in the bottom cooked while food in the top drawer remained cold and wet.

The unit sells for $49.95 by mail or through Sears, Roebuck catalogs. The manufacturer is Wheeler Enterprises, 7855 South 114th St., Seattle, WA 98178.

Building an
Electric Food Dehydrator

Editor's Note: We studied diagrams and plans for several electric food dehydrators before selecting this one, which appeared to be best because of its design and its size. We built it at Garden Way Publishing, tested its operation, then shipped it to the author of this book, Phyllis Hobson, for her to test.

The following information was written by three persons. The first article, describing the construc-

tion of the dehydrator, was written by Dale E. Kirk, agricultural engineer at Oregon State University, as published in the USDA Home and Garden Bulletin 217.

The next section was written by Roger Cota of the Garden Way staff, who built and tested this dehydrator.

Finally, the results of the food tests were written by author Phyllis Hobson.

PLANS FOR A DEHYDRATOR

By Dale E. Kirk

A small dehydrator can be used in the home to preserve many types of fruits, blanched vegetables, meats, and nuts and to make specialty confections from fresh, natural products.

This dehydrator provides 8½ square feet of tray surface, which can accommodate approximately eighteen pounds of fresh, moist product. The necessary heat for evaporating the moisture is supplied by standard household light bulbs, which are efficient and relatively safe heating elements. An eight-inch household type electric fan can be used for air circulation, or a six-inch or eight-inch-diameter air-duct circulating fan may be purchased from an electrical supply house.

The dehydrator box described here is easy to build. It requires only two forms of wood building materials: ½-inch plywood and ¾-inch square wood strips. Construction can be done with a hand saw, a coping saw or compass saw, drill, countersink, screwdriver, and knife. A square or tape is needed for measurements.

The drying trays may be built of wooden slats or metal mesh. We recommend, however, that you purchase prefabricated aluminum window screens for use as trays. They are lightweight, sturdy, easily cleaned, and relieve the builder of much of the more difficult construction.

Construction Materials. You'll need these materials to build the dehydrator described:

1 sheet of ½-inch, 4 × 8 foot, A-C exterior plywood
9 4-foot pieces of 1 × 1-inch nominal (¾ × ¾-inch actual) wood strips
1 8-inch fan
1 set of 5 aluminum screens for trays. *16¾ × 20, 16¾ × 19, 16¾ × 17¾, 16¾ × 16¾, and 16¾ × 15½ inches
1 pair of 2-inch, metal butt hinges
1 ball chain or equivalent door latch
9 porcelain surface-mount sockets
9 75-watt light bulbs
15 feet of asbestos-covered #14 copper wire

---

*Fiberglass treated with nylon or teflon or wood trays may be substituted for aluminum. Do not use galvanized screening material.

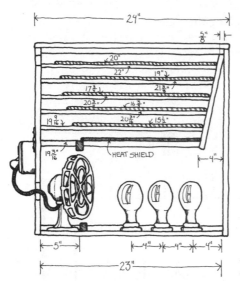

Front and two section views of dehydrator construction.

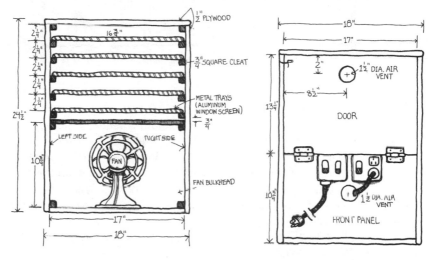

6 feet of #14 wire extension cord, with male plug

1 36-inch length of heavy-duty household aluminum foil wrap

116 1-inch No. 8 flatheat wood screws (nails and glue may be used instead)

18 ⅝-inch × No. 7 roundhead wood or sheet-metal screws

1 10-amp-capacity thermostat, 100-160° F. approximate range

1 4-inch electrical surface utility box with blank cover

2 ½-inch utility box compression fittings

2 wire nuts

Cutting and Assembly. The cutting diagram shows how all of the ½-inch plywood pieces can be cut from the single 4 × 8-foot sheet. It is usually most satisfactory to measure from the factory-cut edges as shown. Allowances for saw kerfs must be made between adjacent pieces.

Cut the plywood sections to size and the 1 × 4 strips to the lengths shown. Then assemble the side panels as shown in the illustration.

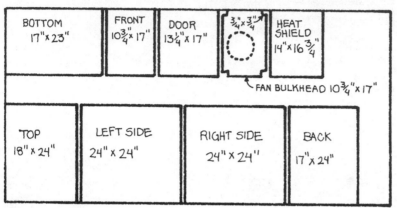

Cutting plan to obtain the necessary plywood parts with a minimum of saw cuts.

Next, lay out the porcelain sockets and fasten to the base, as shown. Fasten the asbestos covered wire to the porcelain sockets. Connect the wire that goes to the yellow screws on the sockets to the thermostat, mounted near the rear on the left side panel. (The yellow screws on the sockets connect to the center pole, rather than the threaded wall of the socket.) Connect the wire that goes to the white screws to the white wire in the extension cord. The third wire (green) in the extension cord should be connected directly to the junction box, mounted on the front panel.

If you use a household-type fan with the base left attached, fasten it in place on the dehydrator base and cut the hole in the fan bulkhead to fit. If you use a duct-type fan, cut the necessary size hole (approximately 8½ inches in diameter for an eight-inch fan or approximately 6½ inches in diameter for a six-inch fan) in the bulkhead and fasten the fan-mounting frame directly to the bulkhead. Now set the bulkhead in place (approximately 5 to 5½ inches from the front panel) and fasten it temporarily in position by two screws through the left side panel as shown. Center the 1½-inch-diameter air vent hole in the front panel directly in front of the fan motor, approximately one inch away from the motor. This will allow the cold air to enter and pass over the motor to cool it.

Next, fasten the right side, back, and top in place.

Cover the heat shield with a heavy-duty household aluminum foil wrap. This provides a reflective surface to protect the plywood heat shield, and also provides a smooth surface on the top of the shield for easier removal of juices that may drip from the drying trays.

You could build the Drying Trays, but we suggest you purchase aluminum window screens made to the sizes listed. You can order these through your local lumber or building supply dealer. If they do not have a ready source of supply, further information about suppliers may be obtained through your local county Extension office. If you prefer to build the trays, we suggest you make a light, wooden frame and use either aluminum screen or galvanized hardware cloth. Most plastic screens will sag badly under load and heat. Black-metal screens will rust and leave stains on the food product.

You'll need some type of adjustable latch to hold the door in a partially opened position during the early stages of drying, when the moisture is being removed rapidly.

As a check on the thermostat setting, some type of thermometer capable of service in the 100 to 160° F. temperature range should be available. The dial type is rugged and easily read. A kitchen-type meat thermometer also will serve. The sensing part of the thermometer should project through the box into the space above the trays for accurate indication of the drying temperature. Placing the sensing element in the heating chamber with the light bulbs will give a misleading, high reading.

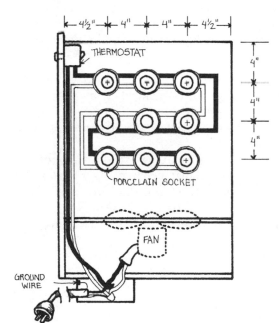

Layout of socket locations and wiring plan.

39

Operation. For most moist fruits and blanched vegetables the trays may be loaded at the rate of one to two pounds of fresh product per square foot of tray surface. The door may be kept closed for the first thirty minutes to sixty minutes to bring the product and the dehydrator box up to the desired drying temperature. Once this temperature is reached, the door should be opened about ½ to ¾ inch at the top to allow easier escape of the moisture-laden air. The moist air will exhaust at the top and additional fresh air will be taken in along the sides of the partially opened door.

Test to see when the first, high-moisture stage is over. Hold your hand at the opening at the top of the door.

When moisture no longer tends to condense on your hand or on your metal watch band, close the door. The air exchange provided by the two 1½-inch-diameter vents should be enough to complete the drying process.

Maintenance. The electric fan motor is supplied by a stream of fresh air from the lower vent, positioned in front of the motor, but it will still operate at a higher temperature than in normal, open-room service. Lubricate the motor bearings with 30-weight engine oil. Lighter grade household or sewing machine oil may tend to gum and stall the fan motor after extended service.

Wash trays with hot water and a detergent when they become soiled with dried-on juices. If you purchased the recommended aluminum window screens with an aluminum wedge strip to hold the screen in place, you can put them in an electric dishwasher without damage.

Alternate Construction and Operation. The dehydrator can be built without a thermostat. Temperature can be controlled by the use of switches to operate various numbers of light bulbs. The diagram shows such a unit, with three separate switches, each controlling three bulbs in the heating chamber.

All three switches should be turned on for at least the first hour or two when the dehydrator is loaded with moist product. As soon as the temperature comes up to the desired level and the extra heat is not needed to warm large amounts of incoming fresh air, one or two switches may be turned off and the drying completed at the reduced heating rate.

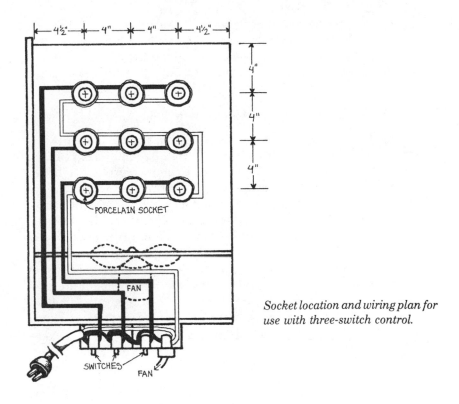

Socket location and wiring plan for use with three-switch control.

BUILDING THIS DEHYDRATOR

By Roger Cota

I like this dehydrator. It's a good basic design—easier to build than I thought it would be when I first glanced at the plans.

The directions plus the illustrations are easy to follow.

Before you decide to build, however, let me tell you two things you should consider:

1. *Parts may be difficult to find.* I spent fifteen hours building this— eight of them finding parts, and seven actually building. (And that doesn't count about an hour spent chewing over the directions and illustrations, just to make certain I understood them.) The most difficult thing to find was the thermostat. We finally bought one from The A-1 Electric & Plumbing Supply Co., Box 66117, Portland, OR 97266 ($13.95 plus $1.50 shipping and handling, plus 15 cents more because I live east of the Rocky Mountains).

2. *The parts are not cheap.* I bought everything except the bulbs, for a total of around $88. You could cut costs if you could scrounge parts such as plywood ($12), the fan ($21), the thermometer ($4.95) or any of the others. If you value your time and have to buy all of the materials, a commercial model, or a kit of one of these, might be a good buy for you.

And here are a few thoughts I had while building this:

The fan I found turns at 3,000 RPM. I don't think that speed is necessary. About 1,700 might be fine. If I were building again, I might even mount a rheostat on the fan, so that I could control those RPM.

We had a surprise with the fan motor. On the first test everything was going smoothly—until the fan quit. We waited. The bulbs of course heated the box quickly, and the thermostat shut them off. Within a minute the fan kicked back in, cooled the box, and the lights came on again. The cycle was repeated a few minutes later. That's when we learned that this motor (and most of the electric motors built today) turns itself off when it shows signs of overheating. This temperature level was reached only when the thermostat was turned to give the hottest conditions in the box. It seemed to make no difference in the functioning of the dehydrator—our test apple dried at just about the same speed as the one in a commercial dryer.

Garden Way staff member Roger Cota, who built this dehydrator, checks the alignment of its five trays.

We added one refinement to our dehydrator—a piece of the tray screen tacked above the fan at the level of the heat shield. You'll see in the illustrations that there's a space there. Food might drop down from a tray being moved and hit the fan—or a finger might stray down and get spanked by the fan.

The thermostat we bought came without a box. We had to fashion a utility box to hold it.

The door on ours fits very smoothly (he said with some pride) but you might want to add a magnetic catch to yours, to hold it in place. They're available at most hardware stores.

Finally, I painted a polyurethene coating over the exterior of the box, to give it a protective coating.

If I were going to build another, I wouldn't build the trays. They can be built of wood, as mine were, but any repair shop that handles screen doors and windows can quickly turn out five aluminum trays that would be dandy—and maybe easier to clean than the ones with wooden sides.

Dale Kirk did a fine job on this design. A lot of thought went into it, to produce a workable dehydrator that even the handyman with little experience can build.

TESTS OF THIS DEHYDRATOR

By Phyllis Hobson

This dehydrator is larger and heavier than any of the commercial models tested. It was too heavy for me to lift up on the kitchen counter, even if it would have fit on my kitchen counter, which it wouldn't.

But it fit nicely on a low table in a well-ventilated utility room, which I had already decided was a better location than the kitchen for an electric dehydrator. I had already decided I liked it because it had two features— deep, sturdy trays and a snug-fitting door. These were two of the most consistent problems I had encountered in the commerical models.

It performed beautifully. On as dry a day as you're likely to find in Indiana in early spring, apple slices and banana chips were crisp in five hours. Without any pretreatment, there was no darkening of pear slices and no loss of flavor in grapes. Unlike many of the commercial dehydrators, it was not necessary to turn the fruit or rotate the trays. All areas of every tray dried evenly.

With the dial set on low and the trays empty, the interior temperature reached 100° F. in ten minutes. With the dial turned to the 110° mark, it reached precisely 110° F. in another ten minutes. It took ten minutes more to reach 120° F.

With the trays filled, it took longer to reach maximum temperature, but the thermostat worked well, adjusting the temperature by turning the lights off, then on again.

I especially liked the trays. With almost an inch of depth, they were easy to handle, even when fully loaded. But I had some problems with the open weave wire mesh because the rough surface made it difficult to remove sticky foods at almost any stage of drying. Not only were the dried foods hard to peel off, but the trays were hard to clean and almost impossible to soak.

In spite of that, I still would use the open wire mesh because it allows for better circulation of air and quicker drying of foods than fine screen. Not only are the trays sturdier than those made of screen, but they will last longer. Those are the reasons I would vote against using aluminum window screens as suggested even though it would be a lot easier on the builder than making wood-framed trays. Under heavy use, screening tends to pull out of aluminum frames with the weight of the food.

I would suggest one change in the trays. Roger Cota followed the directions faithfully for the test model and graduated the length of the trays to fit the sloping tray slots. With every tray one-half inch longer than the tray below it, inserting five different lengths of trays into five different lengths of slots can be a shell game when you have five full trays to load at once. I'm sure the slope is necessary for air circulation and it is possible to mark the trays, but it would simplify construction and use to make all the trays the shorter length.

I have one other suggestion that almost any woman will think of, whether she uses the dehydrator in the kitchen or the utility room. A coat of bright-colored paint or covering of self-sticking contact paper would make the dehydrator more attractive.

44

To Pretreat
or Not To Pretreat

There are as many arguments for and against the need to pretreat fruits and vegetables before drying as there are foods to be dried. After several months of drying foods with and without pretreating, our experiments showed that it depends on the food and the method of drying. Some foods need pretreating. Some don't.

Here are the arguments for and against pretreating, plus some opinions of our own.

FOR PRETREATING

One of the most important substances in any fruit or vegetable is the natural enzyme. It is the catalyst that caused the plant to sprout from a seed, to develop a stem and leaves and finally, fruit. The enzyme causes the fruit to ripen. But the enzyme action doesn't stop when the fruit has ripened, or even when it is picked. Unless it is stopped, the fruit will overmature and finally decay.

Drying foods does not stop enzymatic action. Like freezing, drying only slows it down. Some foods keep well without pretreatment, but others will continue to deteriorate in color, flavor, texture, and nutrients for months after they are dried unless they are treated. Just as in freezing, untreated vegetables tend to become tough and strong-flavored after a period of storage, and without pretreatment, some fruits—such as apples, bananas, peaches and apricots—may darken considerably before and during drying, especially in sun drying. While this darkening in itself does not spoil the fruit, it is an indication that enzymatic action is still at work on the flavor and nutritional value of the food as well as the color.

Vegetables may be pretreated before drying just as they are before freezing, by blanching in boiling water or steam. Blanching is a method of cooking the food for a short time, just long enough to halt the natural enzymatic action. It is a form of quick, incomplete cooking.

Fruits usually are not blanched because it spoils their fresh flavor and their acid content makes the precaution unnecessary. Fruits may be dipped in a solution containing salt, ascorbic acid or fruit juice to prevent darkening. Fruits also may be pretreated with sulfur fumes to keep their color bright.

Instructions for all these methods will follow.

AGAINST PRETREATING

Some people who have years of experience in drying foods claim that pretreating is unnecessary if the foods are prepared properly and dried quickly. They say that foods should be cut into small pieces to expose as much surface as possible to the air and that it is important to have good circulation of air, whether drying is done in the sun or with artificial heat.

Furthermore, they say foods retain more of their natural nutrients and digestive enzymes when they are dried without pretreatment. They argue that blanching cooks the foods and that other methods such as dipping and sulfuring add undesirable chemicals to the foods.

Our choice is to select from the best of both methods. Although it is a good idea to try to keep food drying as natural as possible, some foods require pretreating in order to keep their fresh taste and food values.

Although we do not recommend submitting fruits to sulfur fumes, we have included directions for doing so if you wish. And we agree that results are better with some fruits when they are dipped in fruit juice or an ascorbic acid solution.

Some vegetables, such as peppers and onions, retain their color and flavor best without blanching, but some, such as broccoli, Brussels sprouts, and green, leafy vegetables, fade and become strong-tasting if they are not pretreated before drying. Carrots and other root vegetables may be dried in the sun without pretreating—although they tend to become tough if they are dried in a dehydrator.

PRETREATING METHODS

Blanching is a method of heating the food (usually vegetables) just to the point of inactivating the enzymes without cooking the food through. Steam or water is used. Steam blanching preserves more of the vitamin and mineral values of the food, but requires a longer processing period. It also requires occasional stirring and careful watching to be sure the steam circulates around all the pieces and penetrates them to the center.

Although there is more vitamin loss in water blanching, it requires less time and less special equipment.

Blanching as a pretreatment before drying is much the same as blanching as a pretreatment before freezing. The only difference is that vegetables to be dried should be removed from the pan to drain well, but not plunged into cold water, as is done before freezing. The well-drained vegetables, still hot from blanching, are cut up and placed directly onto the drying trays.

Steam Blanching: Bring to a boil about two inches of water in a steamer, a blanching kettle, or a deep pan with a tight-fitting lid. Place vegetables loosely in a wire basket or colander and spread out as much as possible. Place basket in pan. Vegetables should be above water level, but steam should circulate well through the pieces.

Put a lid on the pan and keep heat high enough for water to boil rapidly. Use a timer and steam length of time specified for each vegetable. For high altitudes add one minute for each 2,000 feet of elevation.

Water Blanching: Fill a blancher or a large pan two-thirds full of water. Bring to a boil. Place vegetables in a wire basket, or a cheesecloth bag or place directly in boiling water. Cover and boil for the length of time specified in the directions. Drain and cut up vegetables. Place on drying trays without chilling. For high altitudes, add ½ minute to the time specified for each 2,000 feet of elevation.

Salt Water Dip: Dissolve six tablespoons flaked pickling salt in one gallon of lukewarm water. To keep fruit from darkening, slice or chop it directly into the water. Allow it to soak no more than five minutes or fruit will absorb too much water and acquire a salty taste. Drain before loading drying trays.

Ascorbic Acid Dip: Ascorbic acid is a form of Vitamin C. Dissolve two tablespoons of ascorbic acid crystals, two tablespoons ascorbic acid powder or five crushed one-gram Vitamin C tablets in one quart of lukewarm water. Slice or chop fruits directly into the solution. When a cup or two of fruit has accumulated in the container, give it a stir and remove the fruit with a slotted spoon. Drain well before loading drying trays.

Fruit Juice Dip: Dip peaches, apples, or banana slices in one quart undiluted pineapple juice or into one quart of lukewarm water into which ¼ cup lemon juice has been stirred. Let fruits remain in the dip no more than five or ten minutes. Drain well before drying.

Honey Dip: Many of the commercially dried fruits sold in health food stores at fancy prices are dipped in a honey solution to retain the color of bananas, peaches, and pineapples. Surprisingly, honey-dipped fruits do not seem to be any sweeter than fruits dried without dipping, although they undoubtedly have more calories.
Prepare the dip by dissolving one cup sugar in three cups hot water. Cool to lukewarm and stir in one cup honey. Dip fruit in small batches and remove with a slotted spoon. Drain well before drying.

Commercial Dip: There are several products on the market designed to be dissolved in water and used as a dip before freezing fruits. The main

48

ingredient of these powders usually is ascorbic acid or sodium sulfite or a combination of the two. Use these products according to the directions on the package, taking care not to let fruits soak more than five to ten minutes or they will absorb too much water. Drain well before drying.

Sulfuring: Although many people object to the addition of sulfur to their food, exposing fruit to sulfur fumes is the pretreatment method preferred for fruit by the U.S. Department of Agriculture. It also is the method often used in drying fruits commercially.

The procedure is simpler than its instructions sound. The important thing to remember is that sulfuring must be done outdoors, and away from the house and from livestock, pets or valuable plant life. Although the odor eventually dissipates, *any fruit that has been sulfured must be dried outdoors, in the sun.* The odor of the sulfur is too overpowering for indoor use in a dehydrator or oven.

To prepare fruit for sulfuring, slice or chop it and spread it out on slatted wood or plastic (not metal) trays. Some fruits, such as apples and peaches, which darken easily, should be dipped in fruit juice or an ascorbic acid solution to prevent darkening before the sulfuring process begins.

When the first tray is filled with fruit, set it to span two concrete or wooden blocks placed several inches apart. They should hold the tray three to four inches off the ground. As each tray is filled, place 1½-inch blocks or spools at the four corners of the previous tray and place the next tray on these to stack them with space in between. Trays may be stacked this way, keeping them 1½ inches apart, until the stack is four to six trays high, but still solid.

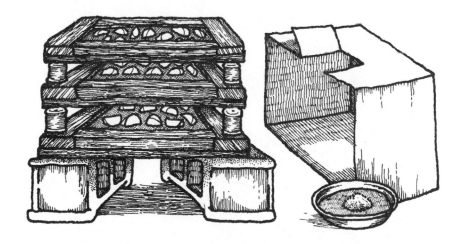

Select a cardboard (grocery store variety) box large enough to cover the stack with at least 1½ inches to spare. Remove the top and turn the box upside down. Using a sharp knife, cut a six-inch door on one side at what is now the bottom (open end) of the box. Cut a six-inch slash at the top. Place the box, open end down, over the stack of trays filled with fruit.

Into a one-pound coffee can or a disposable aluminum pie pan, measure one tablespoon flowers of sulfur for every pound of fruit to be sulfured. Flowers of sulfur may be purchased at most drug stores or where livestock supplies are sold. Don't use garden dusting sulfur. Slide the can containing flowers of sulfur through the six-inch door at the bottom. Light the sulfur with a match, taking care not to leave any burned matches in the sulfur container.

As soon as the sulfur is lit, push the container away from the door to a spot directly under the trays of fruit. For the time being, keep the door and the slash at the top open.

When the sulfur has melted and is burning well, seal around the edge of the bottom of the box, piling up dirt against the box or using rags or small, washable rugs. (Remember, they will smell of sulfur when you are finished.) Leave the door and slash open while the sulfur is burning, then close them tightly and let the fumes circulate through the trays until the fruit is bright and glistening, with a small amount of juice collected in the cavities.

Sulfuring time will depend on the size of the box and the amount of fruit to be sulfured, but most fruits are completed in one to two hours.

The fruit now is ready to be dried. Remember—sulfured fruit must be dried in the sun, not in an oven or dehydrator.

Testing and Storing Dried Foods

Before dried foods are stored, they should be tested to be sure enough moisture has been removed to make it impossible for mold and bacteria to grow and cause decay. Well-dried foods will vary from a moisture content of 5 percent for leafy vegetables such as spinach to 25 percent for juicy acid fruits such as apricots.

All dried foods should be cooled before testing for dryness because warm foods feel more moist than when they are cooled. In general, dried foods feel dry when they are squeezed.

Root vegetables, squash, and pumpkin are dry when they are tough and leathery, still pliable, but with no moisture in the center. Cabbage, broccoli, and celery should be hard and brittle. To test, cut through the center with a knife or take a bite of it.

51

Green beans should be a dark green, with a leathery, "shoe lace" appearance. Greens such as spinach and beet tops should be brittle enough to crumble in the hands. Corn, peas, and dry beans should be dry enough to shatter or split in two when tapped with a hammer.

Fruits are dry when they are leathery enough that several pieces will spring back without sticking together after being squeezed.

Fruits such as peaches, pears, apples, and plums should remain pliable. Others, such as berries, rhubarb, and lemon or orange peel, should be crisp and brittle. Banana slices may be crisp or slightly pliable, depending on the thickness of the slices, the method of pretreatment, and the temperature at which they were dried.

Fruit leathers are still slightly sticky to the touch when they are dried, but will pull away from the plastic wrap easily. For long-term storage, dry leathers until they are no longer sticky.

Extra care should be taken in testing all high-protein foods, particularly meats. They should be very dark colored and fibrous enough to form sharp points at the corners when bent. When dry enough for long-term storage, jerky should be so fibrous it is very hard to chew. As a compromise, many people keep dried meats and jerky tightly wrapped and in the refrigerator or freezer.

Herb leaves are dry enough for storage when they are so brittle they will crumble easily in the hands.

Grains and grain products are best tested for drying by tasting. Well-dried grains will have a nutty taste and a hard, brittle texture. Grain cereals and crackers will be crisp. Noodles will be brittle enough to break in the hands.

When in doubt as to whether a food is dry, remember that it is better to overdry than to underdry.

STORING DRIED FOODS

Dried foods should be stored in small batches in airtight, insect-proof containers. Dried fruits and vegetables may be stored in small glass or plastic jars such as those in which pickles, mustard, instant coffee, and jelly are purchased. After the dried food has cooled, put it inside the container and screw the lid on tightly. Don't delay this step, or the dried produce will begin to accumulate moisture. Jars are free and have the advantage of keeping the dried food visible so it may be checked for moisture the first few weeks of storage. Any sign of moisture beads inside the jar is a signal that the food is not dry enough for storage and should be returned to the drying trays.

Dried meats also may be stored in glass or plastic jars, but the jars should be small because dried meat is a very concentrated food and is used in small amounts. Every time the jar is opened, moisture in the air enters the jar and the food. It should be remembered, too, that dried meats, especially jerky, will keep only for a short period at room temperature because any fat on the meat will turn rancid. A refrigerator or freezer is recommended for long-term storage. Jerky is cut in serving-size sticks, each wrapped in waxed paper or plastic wrap, and sealed in cans or jars.

Large batches of grain may be stored in metal containers such as potato chip or lard cans. One to two cups of the grain should be sealed in plastic freezer bags or brown bags, then stacked inside the can. Different grains may be stored in one can, but don't mix packages of grains and other dried foods in one container. Be careful also not to combine packages of cabbage, onions, broccoli, or fish, or any strong-flavored food, with other foods, for their flavors will blend.

Fruit and vegetable leathers are rolled in plastic wrap or waxed paper. Stand the rolls in a metal or glass container—clean, dry coffee or shortening cans work well—and seal with a tight-fitting lid.

Because their flavors are easily lost, herbs, herb mixtures, and herb teas are best stored separately in very small containers such as clean, dry pill or vitamin bottles. Be certain, though, that the bottles are odor-free. Herb leaves that are to be used within a few months usually are crumbled before storing, but for best flavor retention in long-term storage, herb leaves may be stored intact, then crumbled just before using.

Be sure to label jars and plastic packages with the name of the food and the date it was dried. One good method is to print this information on a piece of masking tape on the outside of the dried food container. Include too on the label the number of servings in the package and—for the more involved dishes such as soups and stews—directions for preparing the food.

For camping trips and backpacking, ready-to-cook soup mixes are best sealed in plastic freezer bags that are lightweight, disposable, and waterproof. For storage in vacation homes, where insects and predators might be a problem, store the freezer bags inside glass or metal containers with tight-fitting lids. Remember, though, that mice can chew through plastic.

Although dried foods can withstand freezing temperatures without harm, they will lose color, flavor and nutrients when exposed to light and heat. *Keep containers in a dark, dry, cool place.* This doesn't mean they need a special storage area. A closed, unheated closet anywhere in the house will serve the purpose. Lacking that, glass jars may be kept dark by inverting a cardboard box over them or covering them with a bushel basket or a sheet of black plastic. Metal containers keep their contents dark.

IF YOU CAN'T
DRY IT RIGHT AWAY

There will be times when the weather is humid or your dryer is overloaded or it just isn't convenient to dry foods at harvest time. When this happens, you can postpone the drying season of some foods.

Apples, pears, onions, celery, squash, pumpkins, carrots, and some other foods may be stored in a cool, dry storage room for a few weeks.

Others, such as kidney and lima beans, green peppers, corn, peaches, and strawberries, may be stored in the freezer until a more convenient time. Pretreat corn and peaches as you would for freezer storage, but the others need no pretreatment. For fruit leathers, puree the fruit in the blender, pour into a container and freeze. When you're ready to dry them, just thaw and spread the puree on drying trays.

Drying
Fruits

Dried fruits are the oldest, the most familiar and the most popular of dried foods. They also are the simplest to dry and the simplest to use.

Pretreatment of fruits before drying may be as simple as a quick dip in salt water or as complicated as the sulfuring process. Pretreatment may be unnecessary when some fruits are dried in a dehydrator.

In order to preserve their fresh taste, blanching—a form of quick cooking—is not recommended for fruits although they may be dipped in fruit juice, salt water or ascorbic acid solution to keep their color from darkening. Directions for these dips are included in the earlier section on pretreating.

55

Directions also are included in that section for sulfuring, a method by which the fruit is subjected to sulfur fumes to preserve the bright color. Although sulfuring is not necessarily recommended, it is included here for those who want to use it. Fruit which has been sulfured may be dried only by the sun drying method. Fruits which have been dipped or left untreated may be dried by any of the three methods recommended, drying in a dehydrator, drying in the sun, or drying in an oven or homemade dryer, specific directions for each are included under each fruit.

Although dried fruits may be cooked in an equal amount of boiling water or refreshed by soaking overnight in water to cover, they are delicious eaten in the dry form, as a snack, or as a quick, concentrated meal.

The following are fruits recommended for drying.

APPLES

Use well-ripened, but still firm fruit with solid flesh and tart-sweet flavor. Wash and core. Peel or not, according to preference. Cut in wedges, then in slices ¼-inch thick, or in ¼-inch crosswise rings.

Dehydrator: Preheat dehydrator to 115° F. Slice apples directly onto dehydrator tray. Spread slices one layer deep on trays, without overlapping slices. No pretreatment is necessary if you work quickly. As each tray is filled, place it in the dehydrator before loading the next tray. Dry 6 to 8 hours, stirring or turning fruit once. After the first 6 hours, test for dryness every 2 hours until there is no moisture in the middle when a slice is bitten.

Sun: Dip slices in water in which ascorbic acid or commercial dip has been dissolved, wet slices with diluted lemon juice (¼ cup lemon juice to 1 quart water) or full-strength pineapple juice. Or sulfur for one hour.

Spread pretreated slices on drying trays. Cover with a layer of cheesecloth and place in a well-ventilated place in full sun.

Every few hours stir them to expose undried sides. Take trays inside at night to protect them from dew. Apples will take 2 to 3 days to dry completely. Well-dried apple slices should be leathery and chewy. To test for dryness, cool a few slices and taste. There should be no crispness in the center.

Oven or Homemade Dryer: Spread apple slices—pretreated or not, according to your preference—over drying trays. Dry 6 to 8 hours at 115°F., stirring slices once, then test every 2 hours until dry.

To Use: Sliced, dried apples are delicious eaten as a snack or they may be used in almost any way cooked apples are used. One cup yields about 1¼ cups cooked or refreshed apples.

RAW APPLESAUCE

Soak 1 cup slices in 1 cup hot apple cider 3 to 4 hours. Puree in blender and serve as you would applesauce.

COOKED APPLESAUCE

Pour 1 cup boiling water over 1 cup dried apple slices. Cover and simmer over low heat about 30 minutes, until apples are soft.

DRIED APPLE PIE

1½ cups boiling water
1½ cups dried apple slices
⅓ cup sugar
½ teaspoon powdered cinnamon

¼ teaspoon ground nutmeg
2 tablespoons butter or margarine
Unbaked 2-crust pastry

Pour boiling water over dried apples and let soak 3 to 4 hours. Add sugar, cinnamon, and nutmeg. Stir well. Fit half of pastry into a 9-inch pie pan and pour apple mixture into this. Dot with butter or margarine cut into bits. Cover with remaining rolled-out pastry and bake 45 minutes in a 350° F. oven. Makes one 9-inch pie.

APRICOTS

Pick or buy apricots when perfectly ripe. Fruit should not be mushy, but green fruit does not dry well. Any size or variety will do, but choose those with a bright orange color and sweet flavor.

To simplify peeling, dip ripe apricots in boiling water for 1 minute, then in cold water 1 minute. Skins will slip off easily.

Cut apricots in half, removing seeds. For faster drying, slice or chop. They will turn quite dark without pretreating. Dipping in ascorbic acid solution, a commercial dip or Honey Dip is recommended. Sulfuring may be used if apricots are to be dried in the sun.

Dehydrator: Spread apricot halves, slices or pieces on dehydrator trays in a single layer. Dry at 115° F. until leathery, with no moisture in centers when cut. Halves will take 36 to 48 hours. Slices will take 12 to 18 hours. Chopped pieces will dry in less time, according to their size. Turn halves or stir pieces occasionally and rotate trays front to back, side to side, and top to bottom once or twice during drying.

Sun: Spread apricot halves, slices or pieces on trays, cut side up. Cover with cheesecloth and place in full sun. Prop up cheesecloth to keep it from touching fruit. Turn or stir pieces occasionally and take in each night to protect from dew. When top side of halves is dried, turn and flatten by mashing with the heel of the hand or by pressing with a block of wood or other flat instrument. Test for dryness before storing. The halves will take 4 or more days to dry in good weather. Peeled slices will dry in 2 days or more.

Oven or Homemade Dryer: Spread apricot halves, slices or pieces on drying trays. Dry at 115° F. until leathery, 2 to 3 days for halves, less time for slices or chopped pieces, stirring pieces and turning halves every few hours. Rotate shelves once or twice a day during drying.

To Use: Eat halves and slices without refreshing, or soak in just enough water to cover 3 or 4 hours or overnight. Chopped pieces may be used in fruit cake or mixed with dried banana slices for a delicious snack food. Halves may be simmered over low heat 30 to 45 minutes and served in a fruit compote. They may be pureed in the blender after soaking or cooking for a delicious apricot sauce. One cup will yield about 1½ cups cooked fruit.

DRIED APRICOT PIE

3 cups dried apricots	¼ cup cornstarch
3 cups boiling water	2 tablespoons butter or margarine
½ cup sugar	Pastry for 2-crust pie

Soak dried apricots in boiling water overnight or simmer in water just until tender. Do not overcook. Drain any remaining liquid into a blender jar and add ½ cup soaked or cooked apricots. Blend to a pulp. Combine sugar and cornstarch in a saucepan. Gradually add pureed apricots, stirring well to dissolve. Cook over low heat until thickened. Remove from heat, add butter or margarine and stir until melted. Add remaining 2½ cups apricots and pour into unbaked pie shell. Cover with top crust or lattice strips. Bake in 350° F. oven 30 to 45 minutes, until golden brown.

BANANAS

Select well-ripened bananas which are firm, but flecked with brown. Peel and cut into thin slices. Dip in ascorbic acid, undiluted pineapple juice or a mixture of ¼ cup lemon juice and 2 cups water. For crisp slices, pretreat in Honey Dip (see pretreating section).

Dehydrator: Spread slices on dehydrator trays one layer deep, without overlapping slices. Dry at 115° F. until leathery or at 125° F. until crisp. They will dry in 6 to 8 hours in dry weather. After 3 to 4 hours, peel slices from trays and turn over. Rotate trays front to back, side to side and top to bottom once during drying.

Sun: Spread pretreated banana slices one layer deep on drying trays covered with cheesecloth. Top with cheesecloth propped up to keep it from touching fruit. Dry in a well-ventilated place in full sun. At the end of the day, turn slices by flipping bottom cheesecloth and take trays inside for the night. They will take 2 or more days to dry.

Oven or Homemade Dryer: Spread slices in a single layer over drying trays, taking care not to overlap slices. Dry at 115° F. 8 to 10 hours, until leathery or crisp, according to preference. Turn slices and rotate trays once during drying.

To Use: Eat banana slices as a confection or combine with dried or fresh apricots, peaches or pineapple. These slices also may be added to cake or cookie batters without being refreshed. One cup yields about 1¼ cups refreshed bananas or 3/4 cup mashed banana.

DRIED BANANA NUT BREAD

¾ cup boiling water	1 teaspoon vanilla
¾ cup dried banana slices	1½ cups all-purpose flour
¼ cup shortening	2 teaspoons baking powder
½ cup sugar	½ teaspoon salt
1 egg	½ teaspoon baking soda
1 cup bran cereal	½ cup chopped nuts

Pour boiling water over dried banana slices. Let soak 1 hour, then process in blender or mash with potato masher. Set aside. In a mixing bowl, cream shortening and sugar until fluffy. Add egg and beat well. Add bran, banana puree, and vanilla. Combine flour, baking powder, salt, soda, and nuts. Add to first mixture, stirring only to blend well. Pour into greased 9 by 5-inch loaf pan and bake in 350° F. oven 1 hour, until a toothpick inserted in the center comes out clean. Makes 1 loaf.

DRIED BANANA FRITTERS

1 cup dried banana slices	½ cup all-purpose flour
1½ cups boiling water	1 tablespoon sugar
1 egg yolk	1 egg white, stiffly beaten
1 tablespoon cooking oil	Hot oil for frying, at least 2 inches deep
¼ teaspoon salt	

Cover dried banana slices with boiling water. Let soak 1 to 2 hours, then drain, reserving any soaking liquid. In another bowl, beat egg yolk. Add oil, salt and ¼ cup reserved soaking liquid or water. Add flour and sugar and beat until smooth. Add slices, another ¼ cup soaking liquid or water and stiffly beaten egg white. Drop batter by tablespoons into oil which has been heated to 375° F. Fry until golden brown, turning once. Sprinkle with powdered sugar. Serves 6.

BLUEBERRIES (cranberries and gooseberries)

Wash firm but well-ripened berries. Cut in half or drop in boiling water 30 seconds to split skins. For added sweetening, they may be dipped in Honey Dip.

Dehydrator: Spread in a single layer on trays and dry at 115° F. until berries are hard, but still chewy. Stir with the hands every few hours and rotate trays front to back, side to side, and top to bottom, at least once. They will dry in 12 to 24 hours.

Sun: Spread berry halves or whole berries in a thin layer over drying trays. Cover with cheesecloth propped to keep it from touching the berries and place in full sun in a well-ventilated area. Stir with the hands occasionally to help dry uniformly. Take trays inside at night. They will dry in 2 to 4 days.

Oven or Homemade Dryer: Spread berries in a single layer on trays. Dry at 115° F. until berries are hard, but still chewy. Stir occasionally and rotate trays once or twice. They will dry in 18 to 36 hours.

To Use: These berries—plain or honey-dipped—are delicious eaten as a confection, alone or mixed with other dried or fresh fruits. They may be refreshed by soaking in an equal amount of water or fruit juice 3 or 4 hours. Use as you would fresh berries. They may be added without soaking to muffins, cakes and puddings. For a pureed sauce, soak or cook 1 cup berries in 1 cup boiling water. Process in a blender. Serve over pudding or ice cream.

DRIED BERRY COBBLER

Filling:

2 cups dried blueberries, cranberries or gooseberries

2 cups boiling water

1 to 1½ cups sugar (depending on tartness of berries)

2 tablespoons tapioca

2 tablespoons butter or margarine

Soak berries in boiling water 3 to 4 hours. Drain any remaining soaking water into blender jar and add ½ cup soaked berries. Process to a fine puree. Arrange remaining berries in a shallow baking pan. To puree in blender, add sugar and tapioca and blend. Pour over berries. Dot with butter or margarine. Cover berries with batter (below) and bake 30 minutes in 400° F. oven. Serve warm with cream or whipped cream. Serves 6.

Batter:

¼ cup butter or margarine

½ cup sugar

1 egg, well beaten

1½ cups all-purpose flour

2 teaspoons baking powder

½ teaspoon salt

½ cup milk

Cream butter and sugar. Add egg. Sift flour with baking powder and salt. Add, one-half cup at a time, alternately with milk.

DRIED BLUEBERRY WAFFLES

1¾ cups all-purpose flour

3 teaspoons baking powder

¼ teaspoon salt

2 eggs

1¼ cups milk

6 tablespoons cooking oil

1 cup dried blueberries

Combine dry ingredients and set aside. Beat eggs with egg beater until light. Add milk and oil, then dry ingredients. Beat until smooth. Fold in dried berries and bake on a waffle iron, following manufacturer's directions. Serves 4.

CANDIED FRUIT

Almost any fruit may be candied. Some of the best are pineapple, cherries, chopped apricots, watermelon rind, and lemon, orange, or grapefruit peel.

Cut pineapple, apricots, or watermelon rind into small pieces. Chop cherries or cut in halves. Remove white membrane from lemon, orange, or grapefruit peel and cut into strips or small pieces.

Combine 1 cup sugar, 1 cup honey and 1½ cups water in a heavy saucepan or iron skillet. Bring to a boil over medium heat and cook to 234° F., stirring constantly. Drop in small amounts of prepared fruits or fruit peels, separately or mixed. Cook over low heat until fruit or rind is transparent, 25 to 30 minutes. Drain and repeat until all fruit is candied.

Dehydrator: Spread candied fruit over trays in a thin layer. Dry 12 to 18 hours, at 120° F. until fruit is no longer sticky and centers have no moisture. Stir occasionally and rotate trays once or twice during drying. Sprinkle with sugar and pack in glass jars or metal tins with tight-fitting lids.

Sun: Line trays with a layer of cheesecloth. Spread a thin layer of candied fruit over this and cover with cheesecloth propped up to keep it from touching fruit. Dry 1 to 2 days, stirring occasionally, until it is no longer sticky.

Oven or Homemade Dryer: Spread candied fruit over trays. Dry at 120° F. 18 to 24 hours, stirring occasionally and rotating trays once or twice until it is no longer sticky.

To Use: Candied dried fruit is especially popular in cookies and fruit cakes around Thanksgiving and Christmas time. Here are two good recipes:

HOLIDAY OATMEAL DROPS

⅔ cup butter or margarine
¾ cup brown sugar, firmly packed
1 egg
1 teaspoon vanilla
2 cups all-purpose flour
2 teaspoons baking powder
½ teaspoon salt

1 cup rolled oats, uncooked
1 cup mixed dried candied fruit, cut
  in small pieces
½ cup shredded coconut
¼ cup milk
48 pecan halves

In a large bowl, cream butter or margarine and brown sugar until fluffy. Add egg and vanilla and beat well. In another bowl, combine flour, baking powder, salt, oats, candied fruit, and coconut. Add, a little at a time, alternately with milk, to creamed mixture. Blend well. Drop by teaspoonfuls onto lightly greased cookie sheet. Press a pecan half into the top of each cookie. Bake 10 to 12 minutes in 350° F. oven. Makes 4 dozen cookies.

GOLDEN FRUITCAKES

4 cups all-purpose flour
2 teaspoons baking powder
1½ teaspoons ground nutmeg
2 teaspoons powdered cinnamon
½ teaspoon salt
2 cups butter or margarine
2 cups brown sugar, firmly packed
12 eggs

1 tablespoon dried lemon peel,
  ground
3 cups coarsely chopped pecans
4 cups dried candied pineapple, cut
  up
3 cups dried candied cherries, cut in
  halves

Combine flour, baking powder, nutmeg, cinnamon, and salt. Set aside. In a large bowl, cream butter or margarine and brown sugar. Add eggs, one at a time, beating well after each addition. Gradually add 2/3 of the flour mixture, blending well. Add dried lemon peel. Add pecans and candied fruits to remaining 1/3 of flour and stir well. Add to batter, all at once.

Spoon into one large greased and floured angel cake pan or 12 greased and floured small, clean soup cans. Fill containers to within 1 inch of the top. Place a shallow pan filled with water in bottom of oven heated to 275° F. Cover large cake loosely with aluminum foil and bake 4½ hours, uncovering last hour. Bake small cakes 1 hour, 15 minutes. With both, toothpick inserted in center should come out clean when cake is done. Cool completely before removing from pan. Makes 1 large or 12 small fruit cakes.

CHERRIES

Wash and pit fully ripe sweet or tart cherries. Drain well. Cut in half, chop or leave whole.

Dehydrator: Spread cut or whole cherries over dehydrator trays and dry at 115° F., stirring occasionally and rotating trays front to back, side to side, and top to bottom at least once during drying. When dry, cherries should be chewy. Whole cherries will take 24 hours or more. Cut cherries will dry in less time.

Sun: Spread cut or whole cherries thinly over trays. Cover with cheesecloth propped to keep from touching cherries. Dry in hot sun in a well-ventilated area, stirring occasionally. Cut cherries will dry in 1 or 2 days. Whole cherries will take 4 to 5 days. Take trays inside at night.

Oven or Homemade Dryer: Spread cut or whole cherries over trays. Dry at 115° F., stirring occasionally and rotating trays once or twice a day, until cherries are chewy and dried through. Whole cherries will dry in 24 to 36 hours.

To Use: Dried sweet or tart cherries are delicious eaten as raisins. They also add taste and eye appeal when used in any recipe for cookies, cakes, bread or puddings in place of raisins. To refresh dried cherries, soak overnight in an equal amount of water. One cup yields about 1¼ cups refreshed fruit.

DRIED CHERRY DUMPLINGS

Sauce:

1 cup dried tart cherries
3½ cups boiling water

½ cup sugar
2 tablespoons butter or margarine

Combine all ingredients in heavy skillet or electric frypan. Bring mixture to a boil, reduce heat and simmer 20 to 30 minutes, until cherries are tender.

Dumplings:

1 cup all-purpose flour
1½ teaspoons baking powder
¼ teaspoon salt
¼ cup sugar

2 tablespoons butter or margarine
½ teaspoon vanilla
½ cup milk

Combine dry ingredients. Cut in butter or margarine with two knives or pastry blender until mixture is crumbly. Add vanilla and milk and stir only enough to moisten flour. Drop by spoonfuls into boiling sauce. Simmer over low heat, uncovered, 5 minutes, then cover and steam gently 15 minutes more. Serve warm with sauce. Serves 4.

DRIED
CHERRY MARMALADE

2 cups dried sweet cherries
2 cups boiling water
1 orange, finely chopped

1 package powdered pectin
3½ cups sugar
2 tablespoons dried lemon peel

In a large pan, combine dried cherries, water, and chopped orange (remove any seeds, but chop or grind peel with orange). Cook over low heat 30 minutes. Remove from heat and add pectin, sugar, and lemon peel. Bring to a boil over low heat, stirring until sugar and pectin are dissolved. Bring to a full, rolling boil and cook 2 minutes, stirring frequently. Pour into hot, sterilized jars and seal. Makes about 2 pints.

CURRANTS

Select red-ripe currants at their sweetest. Wash and drain well. Drop in boiling water 30 seconds to split skins. Drain well.

Dehydrator: Spread whole currants on trays. Dry at 115° F. until shriveled and chewy with no moisture in the centers. Stir occasionally during drying and rotate trays. Currants will dry in 18 to 24 hours.

Sun: Spread whole currants thinly on drying trays and cover with cheesecloth propped so it will not touch the currants. Place trays in a well-ventilated area in full sun. Dry until chewy, stirring occasionally with the hands. Currants will take 2 or 3 days to dry.

Oven or Homemade Dryer: Spread currants in a thin layer over drying trays. Dry at 115° F., stirring occasionally and rotating trays until currants are hard and chewy. Drying will take 24 hours or more.

To Use: Use currants as you would raisins or dried figs, in fruit cakes or any baking. They cannot be refreshed, but should be used in the dry form.

DRIED CURRANT JELLY

3 cups boiling water	3 cups sugar
4 cups dried currants	1 package powdered pectin

Pour boiling water over dried currants and let set 1 hour. Crush currants with a potato masher and bring slowly to a boil in the soaking water. Simmer 20 minutes. Strain juice through jelly bag or three thicknesses of cheesecloth. Discard berries and measure juice. Add water to make 4 cups. Combine with pectin in a jelly kettle or large pan. Bring to a boil and boil hard 1 minute, stirring to dissolve pectin. Bring to a full rolling boil that cannot be stirred down. Add sugar and stir until dissolved. Bring to a full rolling boil again and cook, stirring constantly 1 minute. Remove from heat, skim off foam, and pour into hot, sterilized jelly glasses. Seal immediately. Yields five 6-ounce glasses.

DRIED CURRANT BARS

2 cups all-purpose flour	⅔ cup shortening
¼ teaspoon baking soda	⅓ cup brown sugar
½ teaspoon salt	¼ cup light molasses
1 teaspoon powdered cinnamon	1 egg
½ teaspoon ground nutmeg	2 tablespoons water
½ teaspoon ground allspice	1 tablespoon vinegar
½ teaspoon ground ginger	1½ cups dried currants
¼ teaspoon ground cloves	¾ cup chopped nuts

Combine flour, soda, salt, and spices. Set aside. In another bowl, cream shortening and brown sugar. Add molasses and egg. Stir in water and vinegar. Blend in dry ingredients, currants, and nuts. Spread in greased 10 by 15-inch shallow baking pan and bake in 350° F. oven about 20 minutes, until lightly browned. Cool slightly, then mark off into 2 by 3-inch bars. While still warm, drizzle with thin confectioners' sugar icing. Cool and cut into bars. Makes 20 cookies.

FIGS

Figs should be soft and greenish yellow or purple in color when ripe. They soften and bruise easily, so they should be dried soon after picking. Wash in cold water and drain until dry. For whole figs, blanch in boiling water 30 seconds to check the skins, then drain and blot dry. Or skins may be pierced a few times with a fork. For faster drying, cut figs in half or chop fine. Figs may be steam blanched, dipped in Honey Dip, candied (see below), or dried without pretreating.

Candied Figs: Make syrup by combining 1 cup sugar and 1 cup water. Bring to a boil, stirring well to dissolve sugar. Drop whole figs gradually into the syrup without stopping the boiling. Cook over low heat until they look transparent, about 40 to 50 minutes. Stir occasionally as they cook to keep from sticking. Drain well.

Dehydrator: Thinly spread whole fruit or pieces—untreated, pre-treated, or candied—over dehydrator trays. Preheat dehydrator to 120° F. Dry, stirring fruit occasionally and rotating trays, until figs are chewy and dried through. Pieces take 10 to 12 hours. Whole figs take 36 to 48 hours.

Sun: Spread figs—whole or cut-up, pretreated, or not—thinly over drying trays. Cover with cheesecloth and place in a well-ventilated area in full sun. Drying takes 1 to 6 days, depending on the weather and the size of the pieces. Stir occasionally and take inside at night.

Oven or Homemade Dryer: Spread whole or cut-up figs over trays. Dry at 115° F. until chewy and dry to center, stirring occasionally and rotating trays once or twice a day. Drying will take 2 or 3 days.

To Use: Try dried figs as a confection, in dried fruit mixes or as an ingredient in any recipe calling for figs. Cut-up figs are an excellent substitute for raisins in many recipes.

STUFFED DRIED FIGS

Steam dried figs over hot water 15 minutes. Drain and blot with a paper towel to dry. Split down one side. Stuff with nutmeats, dried pineapple bits or marshmallows. Chill 1 hour or more. Dip in melted chocolate or melted caramel. Chill again. Serve as a candy.

DRIED FIG BARS

1 cup boiling water	2 egg yolks
1 cup dried figs, stems removed and chopped	1 cup sugar
	1 teaspoon vanilla
1½ cups all-purpose flour	½ cup buttermilk
½ teaspoon baking powder	½ cup chopped nuts
½ teaspoon baking soda	2 egg whites, stiffly beaten
½ teaspoon salt	

Pour boiling water over chopped figs. Let stand 10 minutes. Drain. In a small bowl, combine flour, baking powder, soda, and salt. In a large mixing bowl, beat egg yolks and add sugar gradually, beating until light. Add vanilla. Add mixed dry ingredients alternately with buttermilk. Stir in figs and nuts. Fold in stiffly beaten egg whites. Spread in greased 8 by 12-inch baking pan and bake in 375° F. oven 25 minutes. Cut into 48 bars.

GRAPES (raisins)

Any variety of grapes is excellent dried, but should be left on the vine until well ripened. They may be left whole or cut in half for faster drying. Any seeds may be removed as they are cut in half. No pretreatment is necessary for grapes cut in half. Whole seedless grapes should be dipped in boiling water 30 seconds to split the skins.

Dehydrator: Spread grapes over trays and dry at 115° F. until dry through to the center, stirring occasionally and rotating trays once or twice. Drying time will vary from 24 to 48 hours.

Sun: Spread grapes on trays and dry in the sun in a well-ventilated place until wrinkled and dried through. Take trays inside each night and stir grapes often during the day. If birds or insects are a problem, cover with a layer of cheesecloth propped so it does not touch the fruit. They will take 3 to 5 days to dry.

Oven or Homemade Dryer: Spread whole or halved grapes thinly over trays. Dry at 115° F., stirring occasionally and rotating trays, until wrinkled and dry to the center, 48 to 72 hours.

To Use: Dried grapes are a nutritious snack food when eaten alone or combined with any dried fruit mixture. Add them to cookie dough, spice cake or rice pudding. Like any raisins, they may be plumped by soaking or cooking in boiling water, but dried grapes cannot be returned to the fresh grape form.

DRIED GRAPE SAUCE

1 cup brown sugar, firmly packed	4 tablespoons vinegar
½ cup boiling water	1½ teaspoons Worcestershire sauce
1 cup dried grapes, seeded	½ teaspoon salt
2 tablespoons butter or margarine	¼ teaspoon powdered cloves

Add brown sugar to water in saucepan. Simmer 5 minutes, stirring to dissolve sugar. Add remaining ingredients and cook over low heat 10 minutes. Serve as a meat sauce with ham or tongue. Makes 2 cups.

DRIED GRAPE COFFEE CAKE

2 cups all-purpose flour
3 teaspoons baking powder
¾ teaspoon salt
⅓ cup sugar
1 teaspoon powdered cinnamon
⅓ cup shortening

1 egg
½ cup milk
½ cup dried grapes, seeded and chopped
1 tablespoon butter or margarine, melted

Combine flour, baking powder, salt, sugar and cinnamon. Cut in shortening with pastry blender or two knives. Combine egg and milk in a cup and add, all at once, to mixture. Add dried grapes and blend. Spread evenly over bottom of well-greased 8-inch square baking pan and brush with melted butter or margarine. Sprinkle with Crumb Topping and bake 25 to 30 minutes in a 375° F. oven. Serve hot or cold. Makes 8 servings.

Crumb Topping:

3 tablespoons butter or margarine
¼ cup sugar

¾ teaspoon powdered cinnamon
3 tablespoons all-purpose flour

Cream butter or margarine and sugar until fluffy. Add remaining ingredients and blend well.

LEMON OR ORANGE PEEL

Wash lemon or orange peel in hot water and cut into ½-inch strips. Scrape and discard white membrane from inside of peel. Cut peel into pieces. No pretreatment is necessary.

Dehydrator: Spread small pieces of peeling on trays and dry at 115° F. 6 to 8 hours, until crisp, stirring occasionally. Grate by running through a blender or food mill and store in small bottles.

Sun: Spread small pieces of peeling on trays and dry in full sun in a well-ventilated place, stirring occasionally. They should be crisp after 1 day of good drying weather. Grate by processing in a blender or food mill and store in small bottles.

Oven or Homemade Dryer: Spread small pieces of peeling on trays. Dry at 115° F., stirring occasionally, until peel is crisp, 8 to 12 hours. Grate by processing in blender or food mill. Store in small bottles.

To Use: These peels may be used as a substitute for fresh lemon or orange juice in many cookie or cake recipes. They add an interesting touch when sprinkled over fruit salads and whipped cream toppings. One-half teaspoon dried lemon peel will replace 1 tablespoon lemon juice in most recipes.

DRIED ORANGE SUGAR COOKIES

¾ cup sugar

½ cup cooking oil

2 eggs, well beaten

3 tablespoons dried orange peel, grated

2 cups all-purpose flour

2 teaspoons baking powder

½ teaspoon salt

Sugar to sprinkle on tops

Blend sugar and oil. Stir in eggs and orange peel. In another bowl, combine flour, baking powder and salt. Add gradually to sugar–oil mixture, mixing well after each addition. Chill 3 to 4 hours or overnight. On a lightly floured surface, roll out thinly and cut with cookie cutter. Arrange 2 inches apart on greased cookie sheet and sprinkle tops with sugar. Bake in 350° F. oven 10 to 12 minutes, until golden brown around the edges. Makes 2 dozen cookies.

DRIED LEMON PUDDING

½ cup sugar

5 tablespoons all-purpose flour

¼ teaspoon baking powder

⅛ teaspoon salt

2 egg yolks

3 teaspoons dried lemon peel, grated

1½ tablespoons butter or margarine, melted

1 cup milk

2 egg whites, stiffly beaten

Combine ¼ cup sugar, flour, baking powder, and salt. In another bowl, beat egg yolks until light. Add lemon peel, melted butter or margarine, and milk. Beat well. Stir in dry ingredients and beat until smooth. Fold remaining ¼ cup sugar into stiffly beaten egg whites. Fold egg white mixture into batter and pour into a greased 1-quart casserole. Set in a pan of warm water and bake in a 350° F. oven 45 minutes, or until firm and lightly browned. Pudding will have a cake-like layer on top and a lemon sauce on bottom. Cool before serving. Serves 4.

PEACHES

Peel completely ripened peaches by dipping in boiling water 1 minute, then in cold water. Skins will slip off. Cut peaches in half and remove stones. Leave in halves, slice or chop into small pieces. Pretreat with one of the dips in the pretreating section to keep fruit from darkening. If you prefer and the peaches are to be dried in the sun, they may be sulfured according to directions in the pretreating section.

To speed drying, spread halves, skin side down, on trays and dry until they begin to wrinkle. Turn halves over and flatten with the hand, a pancake turner or a block of wood. Continue drying until completely dry to the center.

Dehydrator: Spread halves, slices or pieces of peaches over trays. Dry at 115° F. until leathery, with no hint of moisture when cut or bitten. Dry halves 24 to 36 hours, slices 10 to 12 hours, and small pieces 8 to 12 hours, stirring or turning occasionally and rotating trays once or twice a day. Test before storing.

Sun: Spread peach halves, slices or pieces over trays and cover with cheesecloth which has been propped so as not to touch fruit. Dry in a well-ventilated place in full sun, stirring occasionally and taking trays in at night. When dry, fruit should be leathery and almost stiff, with no hint of moisture in the center. Halves will take 4 to 6 days, slices 2 to 3 days and pieces 1 or 2 days, depending on the weather.

Oven or Homemade Dryer: Spread peach halves, slices or small pieces over trays. Dry at 115° F. until leathery and almost stiff, with no moisture inside. Stir occasionally and rotate trays during the drying period, 10 to 14 hours for pieces, 12 to 16 hours for slices, and 36 to 48 hours for halves.

To Use: These peaches are delicious eaten dry, as a snack. They may be mixed with other dried fruits or refreshed by soaking overnight in an equal amount of boiling water. They also may be simmered 20 to 30 minutes in boiling water to cover. It is not necessary to add sugar, but you may if you wish. One cup yields about 1¼ cups refreshed or cooked peaches.

They may be combined with fresh or canned fruit as a compote. Just mix the fruits, add a cup or two of the juice and let set in the refrigerator 3 or 4 hours or overnight before serving.

DRIED PEACH UPSIDE DOWN CAKE

1 cup boiling water

9 dried peach halves or 1½ cups dried peach slices

2 tablespoons butter or margarine

¼ cup brown sugar, firmly packed

¼ cup shortening

¾ cup granulated sugar

1 egg, beaten

1 teaspoon vanilla

1¼ cups all-purpose flour

1½ teaspoons baking powder

¼ teaspoon salt

Pour boiling water over dried peaches and let soak 3 or 4 hours or simmer 20 to 30 minutes, until tender. Drain, reserving any soaking or cooking liquid. Melt butter or margarine in an 8-inch square baking pan and sprinkle with brown sugar. Arrange drained peach halves or slices over brown sugar. Set aside. In a mixing bowl, cream shortening and granulated sugar until fluffy. Add egg and vanilla and beat well. Combine dry ingredients and gradually add, alternately with ½ cup soaking or cooking liquid, or water, beating until smooth after each addition. Pour over peaches in pan and spread out evenly. Bake in 350° F. oven 35 to 40 minutes, or until a toothpick inserted in the center comes out clean. While still hot, invert onto a serving plate, fruit side up. Cut into nine squares. Serve warm.

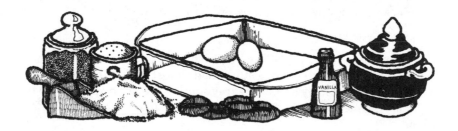

DRIED PEACH RICE PUDDING

½ cup uncooked rice
½ cup sugar
4 cups milk
¼ teaspoon ground ginger

¼ teaspoon salt
1 cup dried peaches, cut into small pieces

Combine all ingredients in a 2-quart casserole. Bake, uncovered, in a 325° F. oven 2½ hours, or until rice is tender. Stir occasionally as it cooks. Cool. Pudding thickens and becomes creamy as it cools. Serves 6.

PEARS

Peel and slice or chop ripe pears which have been softened by wrapping in paper and storing for 2 to 3 weeks. They should be pretreated according to the directions for dips in the pretreating section or will darken badly during drying.

Dehydrator: Spread pear slices or pieces on dehydrator trays. Dry 12 to 18 hours at 115° F. or until slices are leathery, with no moisture in the centers when cut. Stir or turn pieces occasionally and rotate trays once or twice during drying.

Sun: Spread pretreated slices or pieces on cheesecloth-covered drying trays. Cover with cheesecloth which has been propped to keep from touching fruit. Dry in a well-ventilated place in full sun until pieces and slices are leathery, with no moisture in the centers. Pears will dry in 2 or 3 days. At the end of each day, flip bottom cheesecloth to turn pieces over and take inside for the night. Cheesecloth cover can be removed after first day.

Oven or Homemade Dryer: Spread pear slices or pieces in a thin layer over trays. Dry at 115° F., stirring pieces occasionally and rotating trays at least once, for 18 to 24 hours, or until pieces are leathery, with no moisture inside.

To Use: These slices may be eaten as a snack or may be refreshed and used in salads and desserts as you would canned pears. One cup yields about 1¼ cups refreshed or cooked pears.

STEWED DRIED PEARS

2 cups boiling water
1 cup dried pear slices
3 tablespoons sugar

1 teaspoon dried lemon peel, grated
3 whole cloves

Pour boiling water over dried pear slices. Add sugar, lemon peel, and cloves and cover. Simmer over low heat 20 to 30 minutes, until pears are tender. Serves 4.

BAKED
DRIED PEAR SLICES

2½ cups boiling water
1½ cups dried pear slices
½ cup sugar

2 teaspoons dried orange peel, grated
¼ cup frozen orange juice concentrate

Pour boiling water over dried pear slices, sugar and grated orange peel in a 1½-quart casserole. Cover and bake 30 to 45 minutes in a 400° F. oven. Add frozen orange juice concentrate and stir until blended. Chill. Serves 6.

PERSIMMONS

If soft varieties of persimmons are used, dry while still firm. Use riper fruits of round, drier varieties. Peel and cut with stainless steel knife. Cut in ¼-inch slices. No pretreatment is necessary.

Dehydrator: Spread slices on trays without overlapping. Dry 18 to 24 hours, at 115° F. until chewy, with no moisture in center. Stir or turn once or twice during drying and rotate trays.

Sun: Spread slices on trays thinly, covering with a layer of cheesecloth propped so it does not touch the fruit. Dry in a well-ventilated area in hot sun. Persimmon slices will dry in 3 to 5 days, depending on the humidity in the air. Stir occasionally and take trays inside at night. When dry, they will be brown and leathery, but not sticky.

Oven or Homemade Dryer: Spread persimmon slices in a thin layer over trays. Dry at 115° F. 24 to 36 hours, until leathery, with no moisture in the centers. Stir or turn occasionally during drying and rotate trays once or twice.

To Use: Because of their extreme sweetness, dried persimmons are used as a confection, in place of candy, or mixed with other dried fruits such as plums, cherries, and apricots. They may be cut into fine pieces and dried until hard and crisp, then pulverized to a sugar in a blender. Use as you would sugar on cereal or fruit. Use refreshed as you would fresh fruit in puddings, or in cookies in place of dates. One cup yields about ½ cup sugar or 1 cup refreshed fruit.

DRIED PERSIMMON
PUDDING

½ cup boiling water	½ teaspoon baking soda
½ cup dried persimmon slices	¾ cup sugar
2 eggs, well beaten	½ teaspoon salt
1 cup milk	¼ teaspoon powdered cinnamon
1½ tablespoons butter or margarine, melted	¼ teaspoon ground nutmeg
	½ cup dried grapes
1 cup all-purpose flour	½ cup chopped nuts

Pour boiling water over dried persimmon slices. Soak 3 or 4 hours or overnight until softened. Process in a blender or food mill to a smooth pulp. Add eggs, milk, melted butter or margarine and beat well. In another bowl, combine flour, soda, sugar, salt, and spices. Blend into first mixture and beat to a soft batter. Add dried grapes and nuts. Pour into a greased 8-inch square baking pan or casserole dish and bake 30 to 40 minutes in a 350° F. oven. Serve with whipped cream or non-dairy whipped topping. Serves 6.

DRIED FRUIT BARS

1 cup dried persimmon slices
½ cup dried apricot slices
½ cup dried figs
½ cup dried candied cherries, cut in half
1 cup walnuts or pecans, chopped
⅔ cup all-purpose flour

1 teaspoon baking powder
¼ teaspoon salt
½ cup soft butter or margarine
1 cup sugar
2 eggs
1 teaspoon vanilla

Cut dried persimmons, apricots, and figs into small pieces. Combine with cherries, chopped nuts, flour, baking powder, and salt. Set aside. In a large bowl, cream butter or margarine and sugar until fluffy. Add eggs and vanilla and blend well. Add fruit-flour mixture, 1 cup at a time, beating with a spoon after each addition. Spread batter in a greased 9-inch square baking pan. Bake 45 minutes in a 350° F. oven. Cool completely in pan before cutting into 1 by 3-inch bars. Roll each bar in confectioners' sugar. Makes 27 bars.

PINEAPPLE

Cut whole, ripe pineapples into ¼-inch slices. Peel and core each slice. Dry slices whole or cut each slice into wedges or small bits. No pretreatment is necessary, but slices treated in Honey Dip are a delicacy.

Dehydrator: Spread slices, wedges or bits on trays in a thin layer. Dry at 115° F. until chewy and dry to center, 24 to 36 hours. Well-dried pineapple pieces will not stick together when squeezed. Turn slices occasionally or stir pieces once or twice a day. Rotate trays once or twice during drying.

Sun: Spread slices, wedges or bits on trays and cover with cheese-cloth. Dry in a well-ventilated place in hot sun, turning or stirring once or twice a day and taking trays inside at night. Bits will dry in a day or two, wedges will take 2 or 3 days, and slices will dry in 4 or 5 days.

Oven or Homemade Dryer: Spread slices, wedges or bits on drying trays. Dry at 115° F. until chewy and no longer sticky, 36 to 48 hours. Stir or turn pieces occasionally and rotate trays once or twice a day.

To Use: Slices may be refreshed by combining with canned or fresh peaches or pears or by incorporating into gelatin or whipped cream salads. Let set overnight in the refrigerator before serving. It may be used in the dry state by adding cut-up bits to cookie or raisin bread dough or by adding to any pudding recipe before cooking. One cup yields about 1¼ cups refreshed pineapple.

DRIED FRUIT MEDLEY

1 cup dried pineapple slices
½ cup dried banana slices

½ cup dried peach slices
½ cup large flaked coconut

Combine all ingredients. Serve as a finger snack, topped with cream or folded into whipped cream. Serves 6.

DRIED PINEAPPLE SAUCE

2 cups boiling water
1 cup dried pineapple bits
¼ cup sugar

1 tablespoon cornstarch
1 tablespoon butter or margarine
¼ teaspoon salt

Pour boiling water over dried pineapple bits in a bowl. Let cool. In a saucepan, combine sugar and cornstarch. Gradually stir in cooled water with pineapple, stirring well to dissolve. Cook over low heat, stirring constantly, until thickened. Add butter or margarine and salt, cover and cook over very low heat 10 to 15 minutes longer, stirring occasionally. Serve hot over bread pudding or plain cake. Makes about 2 cups sauce.

PLUMS (prunes)

Blue Stanley plums usually are dried commercially for prunes, but any variety of plums is delicious when dried. To dry whole plums, wash and dip 1 to 1½ minutes in boiling water to crack skins. Or, if you prefer, pierce each plum several times with a fork. Do not peel.

For faster drying and for use in dried fruit mixtures, desserts, cookies, and with cereals, slice and seed plums, and cut into small pieces. Plums also may be halved and seeded, partially dried on one side, then mashed with the heel of the hand or a block of wood. The mashed plums are turned over and the drying is completed.

Dehydrator: Spread plums—whole, halved or cut up—on trays and dry at 115° F. stirring pieces and turning whole or half plums every few hours. Rotate trays every 3 or 4 hours. Pieces will dry in 8 to 12 hours; halves will take 18 to 24 hours; whole plums will take 36 to 48 hours or more.

Sun: Spread plums—whole, halved or cut up—on trays in the sun in an area with good air circulation. Stir or turn 2 or 3 times a day. Whole plums will take 4 to 5 days in good weather. Halves will take 3 to 4 days. Slices and pieces will dry in 2 or 3 days. Take trays inside at night.

Oven or Homemade Dryer: Spread plums—whole, halved or cut up—over trays in a thin layer. Dry at 115° F. until hard and chewy, stirring or turning pieces occasionally and rotating trays once or twice a day. Whole plums will take 2 to 3 days, halves from 24 to 35 hours, and pieces 18 to 24 hours.

To Use: Eat cut up plums as a snack alone or mixed with dried peaches, bananas, apricots or other cut up dried fruits. Whole or halved dried plums may be refreshed by soaking overnight in water to cover (the process may be speeded by starting with boiling water) or by simmering 20 to 30 minutes in water to cover. Either cut up or whole dried plums may be chopped and used in any recipe calling for prunes or raisins. One cup yields about 1½ cups cooked plums.

DRIED PLUM DESSERT

1½ cups boiling water
2 cups dried plums, chopped
2 cups rolled oats, uncooked
1 cup all-purpose flour
1 cup brown sugar, firmly packed
¾ cup butter or margarine, melted

1 tablespoon all-purpose flour
½ cup granulated sugar
2 tablespoons dried lemon peel, grated
⅛ teaspoon salt

Pour boiling water over dried plums and let soak 3 or 4 hours or overnight. In another bowl, combine oats, flour and brown sugar. Add melted butter or margarine and mix well. Line bottom of an 8-inch square baking pan with oat mixture, reserving about ½ cup for topping. In a saucepan, combine soaked plums and soaking water, 1 tablespoon flour, sugar, lemon peel and salt. Simmer about 5 minutes, stirring frequently. Remove from heat and pour over oat mixture. Sprinkle with reserved topping. Bake 45 minutes in a 350° F. oven. Serve with whipped cream or non-dairy whipped topping. Serves 6 to 8.

DRIED PLUM DROPS

3½ cups all-purpose flour

1 teaspoon baking soda

1 teaspoon salt

1 cup soft shortening

2 cups brown sugar, firmly packed

2 eggs

½ cup buttermilk or sour milk

Combine flour, soda, and salt. Set aside. In a large bowl, cream shortening and sugar. Add eggs. Stir in buttermilk. Gradually add flour mixture and beat well. Chill 1 hour. Drop by teaspoonfuls about 2 inches apart on a greased cookie sheet. Bake in 400° F. oven 8 to 10 minutes. Makes about 6 dozen cookies.

RASPBERRIES (boysenberries, blackberries, dewberries, loganberries, youngberries)

Wash and dry. No pretreatment is necessary.

Dehydrator: Spread berries in a single layer over dehydrator trays and dry at 115° F. until brittle, stirring berries and rotating trays once or twice during drying. They will dry in 24 to 48 hours.

Sun: Spread berries thinly on drying trays and place in a well-ventilated area in full sun. Cover with cheesecloth if birds or insects are a problem. Stir once or twice a day and take trays inside at night. They will be brittle and well dried in 3 to 4 days.

Oven or Homemade Dryer: Spread berries in a thin layer over trays.

Dry at 115° F. until they are brittle, stirring occasionally and rotating trays every few hours. Drying will take 2 or 3 days.

To Use: Refresh berries by pouring 1 cup boiling water over 1 cup dried berries. Let set 3 to 4 hours or overnight in the refrigerator. For a quick berry sauce, the soaked berries and soaking water may be processed in the blender. Refreshed berries may be used in any way the fresh berries would be used, in pies, sauces, and puddings. Dried berries may be added without refreshing to muffin or cake batter or cookie dough. One cup yields about 1½ cups refreshed berries.

DRIED BLACKBERRY TAPIOCA

2 cups boiling water
½ cup dried blackberries
½ cup sugar
¼ cup quick-cooking tapioca

⅛ teaspoon salt
1 teaspoon dried lemon peel, grated
Cream

Pour boiling water over dried blackberries in a saucepan. Cover and soak 3 to 4 hours or overnight in the refrigerator. Add sugar, tapioca, and salt. Cover and cook 10 to 12 minutes, stirring constantly, until tapioca is cooked. Remove from heat and add lemon peel. Chill. Serve with cream. Serves 4.

DRIED RASPBERRY CAKE TOPPING

⅓ cup boiling water
⅓ cup dried raspberries
2 egg whites
1 teaspoon dried lemon peel, grated

1⅓ cups sugar
1 white or yellow cake, baked in an 8 by 12-inch pan

Pour boiling water over dried raspberries. Let soak 3 to 4 hours or overnight in refrigerator. Add remaining ingredients in a deep bowl and beat with hand beater or electric mixter until light and stiff enough to stand in peaks. Spread over top of cooled cake. Serve immediately. Serves 12.

RHUBARB

Thinly slice or chop tender, rosy-red rhubarb stalks. Do not peel. No pretreatment is necessary before drying rhubarb which will be used in pies or sauce. For rhubarb to be used as a snack or in dried fruit mixtures, glaze slices with Honey Dip before drying.

Dehydrator: Spread slices or pieces—plain or honey dipped—thinly over trays. Dry until hard, 8 to 12 hours at 115°F. Pieces should be stirred occasionally and trays rotated at least once during drying.

Sun: Spread thin slices or pieces in a single layer over trays and place in a well-ventilated place in full sun. Honey-dipped slices should be covered with cheesecloth which is propped up to keep it from touching the fruit. Dry until hard, 1 to 2 days in good weather.

Oven or Homemade Dryer: Spread cut up rhubarb in a thin layer over drying trays. Dry at 115° F. until hard, stirring fruit and rotating trays occasionally. Drying will take 12 to 18 hours.

To Use: Refresh rhubarb by adding 1 cup boiling water to 1 cup dried pieces. Let set 3 to 4 hours or overnight. To make rhubarb sauce, add 3/4 cup sugar and cook over low heat until fruit is soft. One cup yields about 2 cups cooked or refreshed rhubarb.

DRIED RHUBARB PIE

2 cups boiling water
1½ cups dried rhubarb slices
Pastry for 2-crust pie
2 eggs

1½ cups sugar
¼ cup all-purpose flour
¼ teaspoon salt

Pour boiling water over dried rhubarb slices and soak overnight. Line a pie pan with one half of pastry dough and roll out remainder and cut into strips. To assemble pie, combine eggs, sugar, flour and salt. Add refreshed rhubarb and mix well. Pour into pie shell and dot with butter or margarine. Top with pastry strips woven into a lattice design. Bake 15 minutes in a 450° F. oven. Lower heat to 350° F. and bake 30 minutes longer, or until lightly browned.

DRIED RHUBARB BETTY

1½ cups boiling water
1½ cups dried rhubarb
3 cups soft bread crumbs
1 teaspoon dried orange peel, grated

3 tablespoons orange juice
¼ cup honey
½ cup sugar

Pour boiling water over dried rhubarb pieces and soak overnight. Put 1 cup bread crumbs in 1½-quart casserole. In layers, add one half the rhubarb, one half the orange peel and juice and all the honey. Top with 1 cup crumbs and cover with remaining rhubarb, orange peel, and juice, then sugar, in that order. Top with remaining 1 cup crumbs. Cover and bake 45 minutes in 350° F. oven. Serves 4.

STRAWBERRIES

Pick strawberries at the peak of flavor, when they are well ripened, but still firm. Slice. No pretreatment is necessary for drying, but slices may be glazed with Honey Dip for a delicious confection.

Dehydrator: Spread slices thinly over dehydrator trays and dry at 115° F. turning slices after the first 4 hours and rotating trays after 6 to 8 hours. They will dry in 12 to 18 hours, and should be hard when dry.

Sun: Spread slices on trays and cover with cheesecloth propped to keep it from touching fruit. Place in a well-ventilated area in full sun and dry until slices are hard, with no moisture in the center when cut. Turn slices occasionally and take trays inside at night. Will dry in 1 or 2 days.

Oven or Homemade Dryer: Spread slices thinly over drying trays. Dry at 115° F. until hard, 18 to 24 hours, stirring occasionally and rotating trays once or twice.

To Use: These berries, plain or honey dipped, are delicious eaten as a confection alone or mixed with other dried fruits such as bananas and pineapple. Dried strawberries may be refreshed and used in any dish in place of fresh strawberries. Chopped, dried strawberries may be added to cookie and cake batters, puddings, and muffins. A strawberry sauce may be made by processing refreshed strawberries in the blender. One cup yields about 1¼ cups refreshed berries.

DRIED STRAWBERRY
TOPPING

1 cup boiling water
1 cup dried strawberries
1 small package strawberry gelatin

½ cup whipped cream or non-dairy whipped topping

Pour boiling water over dried strawberries and soak 3 or 4 hours or overnight in the refrigerator. Drain, reserving both berries and any remaining soaking liquid. Add water to liquid to make 2 cups. Add gelatin and heat until gelatin is dissolved. Add refreshed strawberries and chill until almost set. Fold in whipped cream or non-dairy whipped topping and serve on squares of cake.

DRIED STRAWBERRY
SHERBET

¾ cup boiling water

¾ cup dried strawberries

⅔ can sweetened condensed milk

2 tablespoons lemon juice

2 egg whites, stiffly beaten

Pour boiling water over dried strawberries and simmer, covered, over low heat 20 to 30 minutes, until strawberries are soft. Press through a sieve, discarding strawberry pulp and seeds and reserving liquid. To the juice, add condensed milk and lemon juice. Chill. Fold in stiffly beaten egg whites. Freeze until firm in ice cube trays. Serves 4.

Drying Vegetables

To obtain the best flavor and nutrition in dried vegetables, pick or buy the crispest, most flavorful fresh vegetables. Drying can preserve much of the nutrition and good taste of vegetables, but it cannot improve on the original food.

Vegetables may be dried by any of three methods recommended for fruits. Artificial heat should not go above 120° F. More care must be taken in pretreating and drying vegetables, because low-acid vegetables are more susceptible to spoilage than acid fruits. Blanching is necessary to keep most vegetables from overmaturing during storage. Careful drying and inspection before storing is also necessary. During storage, dried vegetables should be checked for moisture once or twice a week the first few weeks. One small piece still moist inside can cause the entire batch to mold. This is a reason why vegetables should be stored in small batches.

Most dried vegetables are best cooked without soaking in order to restore their fresh taste and texture. No salt should be added to the cooking or soaking water, however, since salt retards the water absorption of the vegetable. Exceptions are beans and sprouts. Beans usually are soaked before cooking. Sprouts are enjoyed for their dried crispness. Sliced parsnips, tomatoes, turnips, and zucchini are delicious eaten in the dry form as snacks in addition to their use as a cooked vegetable.

ASPARAGUS

Asparagus spears should snap off easily at ground level when ready to pick. During warm spring weather they may have to be picked twice a day or more to keep them from growing too tall. Dry as soon after picking as possible. Wash, drain dry, and cut in ½-inch slices or split lengthwise down the middle. Steam blanch 5 minutes or water blanch 3 minutes. Blot dry immediately with paper towels, but do not chill in water.

Dehydrator: Spread slices or halves thinly over dehydrator trays. Dry at 120° F. 4 to 6 hours. Stir pieces and turn over halves. Rotate trays. Continue drying until brittle. Will dry in 8 to 10 hours, depending on thickness of pieces.

Sun: Spread pieces or split spears on trays. Dry in a well-ventilated area in hot sun until brittle, 1 to 2 days, stirring occasionally and taking in at night to protect from dew.

Oven or Homemade Dryer: Spread pieces or halves on drying trays. Dry at 120° F. 10 to 12 hours, stirring or turning pieces, until brittle and dry through.

To Use: Small pieces give excellent flavor to soups. Add to simmering stock without refreshing. To cook as a vegetable, pour 1 cup boiling water over 1 cup asparagus spears or pieces. Cover and simmer 30 to 40 minutes, until tender. One cup will yield about 1½ cups cooked asparagus.

MARINATED DRIED ASPARAGUS

½ cup salad oil

4 tablespoons lemon juice

1 tablespoon minced dried celery

1 dried bay leaf

½ teaspoon dried chives, minced

1 sprig dried thyme

½ teaspoon salt

½ teaspoon paprika

12 to 18 dried split asparagus spears

Combine all ingredients except asparagus in a jar. Shake until well blended. Pour over dried asparagus in serving dish and refrigerate overnight. Remove bay leaf and thyme before serving. Serves 4 to 6.

SCALLOPED DRIED ASPARAGUS

1 cup boiling water

1 cup dried asparagus pieces

1 tablespoon dried pimiento, diced

3 tablespoons butter or margarine

3 tablespoons all-purpose flour

½ teaspoon salt

1 cup milk

2 hard-cooked eggs, shelled and sliced

¼ cup dried cheese, grated

Pour boiling water over dried asparagus pieces and chopped pimiento. Simmer 30 to 40 minutes, until tender. Drain, reserving liquid. In another saucepan, melt butter or margarine and blend in flour and salt. Gradually stir in milk and cooking liquid. There should be 1½ cups liquid in all. Cook over low heat, stirring constantly until smooth and thickened. Carefully stir in drained asparagus and pimiento and hard-cooked egg slices. Sprinkle top with grated dried cheese. Bake 30 to 45 minutes in 350° F. oven until lightly browned. Serves 4 to 6.

BEANS (navy, kidney, butter, great northern, lima, lentils and soybeans)

Wet beans, shelled from green pods, are difficult to dry satisfactorily and should not be attempted by the beginner. Leave bean pods on the vine in the garden until the beans inside rattle. When the vines and pods are dry and shriveled, pick and shell beans. No pretreatment is necessary. (See also Green Beans.)

Dehydrator: Spread partially dried beans in a single layer on trays. Stirring every few hours, dry at 120° F. until so dry they will split when tapped with a hammer.

Sun: Spread partially dried beans in a thin layer over trays and place in a well-ventilated place in hot sun. Dry 1 or 2 days, until dry enough to split when tapped with a hammer. Stir occasionally and take inside at night. To destroy any insect eggs which may have been deposited during drying, heat in 125° F. oven for 30 minutes before storing. Or store sealed containers in the freezer 2 or 3 days.

Oven or Homemade Dryer: Spread partially dried beans over trays. Dry at 120° F. until they can be split with a hammer, stirring occasionally and rotating trays once or twice.

To Use: These may be refreshed before cooking by soaking 3 to 4 hours or overnight in water to cover. To speed the soaking process, start with boiling water. To reduce the gas-producing properties of beans, drain soaking water and pour fresh water to cover the soaked beans. Cover and bring to a boil over medium heat. Simmer over low heat 30 minutes and drain again. Cook until tender in fresh water. One cup will yield about 2 cups cooked beans.

<h2 style="text-align:center">BAKED
DRIED LIMA BEANS</h2>

3 cups boiling water

1½ cups dried lima beans

4 slices bacon, chopped

2 tablespoons flour

1½ cups canned tomatoes

3 tablespoons dried celery, chopped

¼ cup dried onion, minced

2 tablespoons dried green pepper, diced

¼ teaspoon dried garlic, minced

2 teaspoons salt

Dash pepper

Pour boiling water over dried beans. Cover and cook until tender, 2 to 3 hours in a saucepan, or 35 to 40 minutes in a pressure pan. (Beans also may be cooked by soaking overnight in the water, then cooking 8 to 10 hours in an automatic crockery cooker.) Drain, reserving liquid to use in soup. Place beans in 1½-quart casserole. Sauté chopped bacon in a small skillet. Stir in flour. Add tomatoes, celery, onion, green pepper, garlic, salt and pepper. Cook over low heat, stirring constantly until thickened (15 to 20 minutes). Pour over cooked beans. Cover and bake in 300° F. oven 1 hour. Serves 4.

DRIED KIDNEY BEAN
SALAD

3 cups boiling water	¼ teaspoon sugar
1½ cups dried kidney beans	¼ teaspoon paprika
1 peeled garlic clove	Pepper to taste
3 tablespoons vinegar	½ cup salad oil
2 teaspoons salt	Lettuce
1 teaspoon dry mustard	

Pour boiling water over dried beans. Cover and cook until tender, 2 or 3 hours. Drain, saving liquid for soups. Chill beans in refrigerator. Meanwhile, crush garlic with a fork in a wooden bowl. Add vinegar and let set 10 minutes. Remove garlic and add salt, mustard, sugar, paprika, pepper and salad oil. Beat until blended. Add chilled, cooked kidney beans and mix lightly. Cover and chill several hours, tossing occasionally with a fork. Serve on lettuce leaves. Serves 6.

BEETS

Wash whole beets and cut off tops, leaving 1-inch stubs. Cook in water to cover just until skins will slip off (30 to 35 minutes in a saucepan or 10 to 15 minutes in a pressure pan). Cut off tops and roots and slip off skins. Chop, grate or cut into 1/8-inch slices.

Dehydrator: Spread beets sparsely over trays. Dry at 120° F. until hard, about 8 to 10 hours for slices, 4 to 6 hours for chopped and grated pieces. Turn slices or stir pieces occasionally during drying and rotate trays at least once.

Sun: Spread sliced, chopped or grated beets over trays. Place in a well-ventilated area in hot sun. Dry, stirring occasionally, and taking trays inside at night, until hard. In dry weather slices will dry in 2 or 3 days, pieces in 1 to 2 days. Cover with cheesecloth if birds are a problem, but this will lengthen drying time.

Oven or Homemade Dryer: Spread beets in a thin layer over trays. Dry at 120° F. until hard, 10 to 12 hours for slices, 6 to 8 hours for chopped or grated pieces. Stir occasionally and rotate shelves once or twice during drying.

To Use: These slices may be eaten as a snack alone or with a cheese dip. For a cooked vegetable, cook slices in boiling water 30 to 40 minutes, add butter or margarine and serve hot. Chopped or grated beets may be cooked in boiling water 20 to 30 minutes over low heat. One cup beets will yield about 2 cups cooked vegetables.

DRIED HARVARD BEETS

1 cup boiling water	1 tablespoon cornstarch
1 cup dried chopped beets	½ cup vinegar
⅓ cup sugar	2 tablespoons butter or margarine
½ teaspoon salt	1 teaspoon dried onion, minced

Pour boiling water over dried beets in a saucepan. Cover and cook over low heat 30 to 40 minutes, until tender. Meanwhile, blend sugar, salt, and cornstarch in a saucepan. Add vinegar and stir until well mixed. Cook over very low heat until smooth and thickened, stirring constantly. Add butter or margarine, onion, and beets. Cook over very low heat 15 to 20 minutes to blend flavors, stirring frequently. Serves 6.

BROCCOLI

Pick or buy crisp, dark green broccoli while the buds are small and tightly closed. Do not attempt to dry any that has grown limp or on which the buds have begun to open. Trim stalks, wash thoroughly, and soak in salt water (1 teaspoon salt to 1 quart water) 10 minutes to remove any insects or insect eggs. Rinse again. Split stalks lengthwise in pieces no more than ½-inch thick and blanch in boiling water 2 minutes or in steam 3½ minutes. Do not plunge in cold water, but drain on paper toweling 2 minutes, then cut into 2- or 3-inch pieces or chop.

Dehydrator: Spread pieces over trays in a thin layer. Dry at 120° F. 12 to 18 hours, until crisp, stirring small pieces and turning over large pieces. Rotate trays at least once during drying. Check for moisture in the center by cutting a cooled piece in the middle.

Sun: Spread pieces over trays and place trays in a well-ventilated area in full sun. Stir and turn pieces every few hours. Dry 1 to 2 days, taking inside at night. Test for moisture in the center before storing by cutting a cooled piece in the middle.

Oven or Homemade Dryer: Spread broccoli over trays. Dry at 120° F. until crisp, 18 to 24 hours, turning pieces and rotating trays occasionally during drying.

To Use: Pour 1 cup boiling water over 1 cup broccoli. Cover and cook just until tender. Serve as you would fresh. One cup yields about 2 cups cooked broccoli.

BROCCOLI SOUFFLÉ

1 cup boiling water	½ teaspoon salt
1 cup dried broccoli pieces	1 cup milk
2 tablespoons butter or margarine	3 eggs, separated
4 tablespoons all-purpose flour	

Pour boiling water over dried broccoli. Cover and cook over low heat 30 to 40 minutes, until tender. Drain, reserving liquid for soups. In a saucepan, melt butter or margarine and stir in flour and salt. Gradually add milk, stirring well. Cook over low heat, stirring constantly until well thickened. Beat egg yolks until thick and lemon colored. Stir into thickened mixture. Add chopped, well-drained, cooked broccoli. Beat egg whites until stiff and fold in. Pour mixture into ungreased casserole. Bake in 325° F. oven 30 to 45 minutes. Serves 4 to 6.

DRIED
VEGETABLE TRIO

2 cups boiling water
½ cup dried broccoli pieces
½ cup dried carrots, sliced

6 or 8 dried cauliflower pieces
½ teapoon salt
2 tablespoons butter or margarine

Pour boiling water over broccoli, carrots and cauliflower. Cover and cook until vegetables are tender, 30 to 40 minutes. Lift vegetables out of liquid onto a serving dish. Add salt and butter or margarine to liquid and cook until butter or margarine is melted and liquid has cooked down to ½ cup. Pour over vegetables. Serves 6.

BRUSSELS SPROUTS

Cut Brussels sprouts in half. Steam blanch 6 to 7 minutes or blanch in water 3 to 5 minutes. Drain, but do not chill in cold water.

Dehydrator: Spread halves, cut side up, on trays in a single layer. Dry at 120° F. 8 to 9 hours. Turn halves over. Rotate trays. Resume drying for another 8 or 9 hours. Check for moisture by cooling and cutting through the center with a knife. They should be brittle.

Sun: Spread halves over trays, cut side up. Dry 2 to 3 days in full sun, turning once a day and taking trays inside at night. Dry until brittle and dry to the center. Check for moisture by cutting a cooled piece down the middle. If there is any moisture, dry 1 more day.

Oven or Homemade Dryer: Spread halves over drying trays, cut side up. Dry at 120° F. until crisp, turning pieces occasionally and rotating trays. Drying will take 18 to 24 hours.

To Use: Pour 1½ cups boiling water over 1 cup sprouts. Cover and simmer over low heat 30 to 40 minutes, until tender. Use as you would fresh or frozen sprouts. One cup dried yields about 2 cups cooked vegetable.

94

SCALLOPED
BRUSSELS SPROUTS

1 cup boiling water
1 cup dried Brussels sprouts
2 tablespoons butter or margarine, melted
3 tablespoons flour

¼ teaspoon salt
1 cup milk
½ cup dried bread crumbs
2 tablespoons butter or margarine

Pour boiling water over Brussels sprouts. Cover and cook over low heat 30 to 40 minutes. Drain, reserving liquid. In another pan, melt 2 tablespoons butter or margarine. Blend in flour and salt and gradually stir in milk and reserved cooking liquid. Cook, stirring constantly, until smooth and thickened. Put cooked Brussels sprouts into casserole and pour sauce over. Top with bread crumbs which have been mixed with remaining 2 tablespoons butter or margarine. Bake in 350° F. oven until lightly browned, about 25 minutes. Serves 4 to 6.

FRENCH FRIED
BRUSSELS SPROUTS

1 cup boiling water
1 cup dried Brussels sprouts
1 egg, well beaten

½ cup dried bread crumbs
¼ teaspoon salt
Hot oil for frying

Pour boiling water over Brussels sprouts in a saucepan. Cover and cook over low heat 30 to 40 minutes, until tender. Drain, reserving any liquid for soup. Dip cooked Brussels sprouts first in beaten egg, then in combined bread crumbs and salt. Fry in hot oil until lightly browned, about 3 minutes. Serves 4 to 6.

CABBAGE

Select solid, heavy cabbage heads with fresh, green color. Remove any tough outer leaves and cut heads into quarters. Core each quarter and shred by cutting into strips lengthwise. Blanch in steam 2 to 3 minutes or in boiling water 1½ to 2 minutes. Do not chill in cold water. Drain well.

Dehydrator: Spread shreds thinly over trays. Dry 12 to 15 hours at 120°F., until brittle. Every 3 to 4 hours stir with the hands and rotate trays.

Sun: Spread shreds thinly over trays and place in hot sun where there is good circulation. Dry 2 to 3 days, until crisp, stirring occasionally, and taking trays inside at night.

Oven or Homemade Dryer: Spread shreds in a thin layer over trays. Dry at 120°F. 18 to 24 hours, stirring occasionally and rotating trays once or twice. Dried cabbage should be brittle.

To Use: Drop shreds into boiling soup and allow to cook as the soup simmers. To use as a vegetable, pour 1 cup boiling water over 1 cup shreds and simmer 40 minutes, until tender. One cup yields about 1½ cups cooked vegetable.

DEVILED DRIED CABBAGE

2 cups boiling water

2 cups dried cabbage

1 teaspoon prepared mustard

½ teaspoon salt

1 teaspoon sugar

3 tablespoons butter or margarine

1 tablespoon lemon juice

Pour boiling water over dried cabbage in a saucepan. Cover and cook 30 to 40 minutes, until tender. Mix remaining ingredients in another pan. Heat slowly, stirring to blend. Pour over hot cabbage, mixing lightly. Serves 6.

SWEET AND SOUR
DRIED CABBAGE

2 cups dried cabbage

1 cup dried apple slices

2 tablespoons butter or margarine, melted

2 cups boiling water

2 tablespoons flour

1½ teaspoons dried lemon peel, grated

4 tablespoons brown sugar

Salt and pepper

Add dried cabbage and apple slices to melted butter or margarine in skillet. Add boiling water, cover, and simmer until cabbage and apples

96

are tender, 30 to 40 minutes. Sprinkle with flour. Add lemon peel and sugar and stir well. Salt and pepper to taste. Cover and simmer 5 minutes longer. Serves 6.

CARROTS

Dry young, tender carrots. Scrape or scrub with a stiff vegetable brush. Cut off tops. Cut in ⅛-inch slices or chop into small pieces. Steam blanch 3 to 4 minutes or water blanch 2 to 3 minutes.

Dehydrator: Spread slices or pieces one layer deep over trays. Dry 12 to 18 hours at 120° F. until tough and leathery, with no moisture in the centers. Stir pieces and rotate trays occasionally.

Sun: Spread slices or pieces in a thin layer over trays. Place in a well-ventilated area in hot sun and dry 2 to 3 days, stirring occasionally and taking trays inside at night. Dried carrots should be leathery and pliable.

Oven or Homemade Dryer: Spread pieces thinly over trays. Dry at 120°F. 18 to 24 hours, until pieces are leathery and pliable, stirring occasionally and rotating trays 2 or 3 times.

To Use: Add 1 cup boiling water to 1 cup slices or pieces and simmer 35 to 45 minutes until tender. Serve buttered or creamed. One cup will yield about 1¼ cups cooked carrots.

DRIED CARROT RING

1 cup boiling water	2 eggs, well beaten
1 cup dried carrots	1 tablespoon all-purpose flour
1 teaspoon dried onion, minced	1 cup light cream
2 tablespoons butter or margarine, melted	Salt and pepper

Pour boiling water over dried carrots and dried onion in saucepan. Cover and cook until tender, 35 to 45 minutes. Mash with potato masher or process in blender until smooth. Add remaining ingredients, one at a time, beating well after each addition. Pour into buttered ring mold and place in shallow pan of hot water. Bake 40 to 50 minutes in 350°F. oven until set. Unmold and serve filled with a green vegetable. Serves 6.

DRIED CARROT PATTIES

2 cups chopped dried carrots
2 cups boiling water
2 tablespoons butter or margarine
1 egg, well beaten

½ teaspoon ground nutmeg
½ teaspoon salt
1 cup dried bread crumbs
Hot oil for frying

Cook carrots in boiling water 35 to 40 minutes until tender. Drain. Add butter, egg, nutmeg, and salt to cooked carrots. Combine well and mash with potato masher or electric mixer. Shape into patties and coat with bread crumbs. Chill thoroughly. Fry in hot oil until golden brown. Serves 6 to 8.

CAULIFLOWER

Select firm, white heads of cauliflower with tight, well-formed flowerettes. Soak 10 minutes in a solution of 1 teaspoon salt to 1 quart water to remove insects. Cut in half, slice, or chop. Blanch halves in boiling water 3 to 4 minutes or steam blanch 5 minutes. Slices or pieces should be water-blanched 1 to 2 minutes or steam-blanched 3 minutes. Drain, but do not chill in cold water.

Dehydrator: Spread flowerettes or pieces on trays and dry at 120°F. until pieces are crisp and halves are leathery and dry to the center. Turn halves and stir pieces once or twice during the drying period, 12 to 15 hours for small pieces and 18 to 24 hours for halves.

Sun: Spread cauliflower halves or pieces on trays. Place in full sun where there is good air circulation. Dry 1 to 2 days for small pieces, 2 to 3 days for halves, turning halves and stirring pieces every few hours. Take trays inside at night. When dry, small pieces should be crisp and larger ones should be leathery.

Oven or Homemade Dryer: Spread pieces over trays. Dry at 120°F. 18 to 24 hours for small pieces, 24 to 36 hours for halves, or until pieces are crisp and halves are leathery. Stir occasionally and rotate trays, front to back, side to side and top to bottom, every 4 to 6 hours.

To Use: Cover pieces with boiling water, place over medium heat and bring to a boil. Cover and cook 45 to 50 minutes until tender. Or drop thin slices or small pieces in boiling water or soup broth and cook 20 to 30 minutes. One cup yields about 1½ cups cooked vegetable.

DRIED CAULIFLOWER IN
TOMATO SAUCE

1½ cups dried cauliflower pieces	½ teaspoon salt
1½ cups boiling water	1½ tablespoons dried onion, minced
2 tablespoons butter or margarine	1½ cups water
2 tablespoons flour	1½ cups dried tomatoes

Cook cauliflower in boiling water until tender, 45 to 50 minutes. Meanwhile, melt butter or margarine in saucepan. Stir in flour and add salt, dried onion, 1½ cups water and dried tomatoes. Cook, stirring constantly, until thickened, then cover and cook over very low heat until tomatoes and onions are tender and sauce is smooth. Add cooked cauliflower and serve. Serves 6.

FRENCH FRIED
CAULIFLOWER

1½ cups boiling water	5 cups corn flakes
1½ cups dried cauliflower flowerette halves	2 eggs, well beaten
	2 tablespoons cold water
8 ounces American cheese	Hot oil for frying
1 cup milk	

Pour boiling water over dried cauliflower. Cover and cook 45 to 50 minutes, until tender. Drain. Melt cheese in the top of a double boiler. Gradually add milk, stirring constantly until smooth. Keep hot. Meanwhile crush corn flakes into fine crumbs (or use dried bread crumbs). Combine eggs and 2 tablespoons cold water. Roll cauliflower halves in crumbs, then dip in egg mixture, then back in crumbs again. Fry in hot oil until lightly browned. Drain. Serve with hot cheese sauce. Serves 6.

CELERY

Wash and trim celery stalks. Cut off leaves and dry according to instructions under herbs. Cut stalk in very thin slices. Do not blanch.

Dehydrator: Spread slices in a thin layer over trays and dry 12 to 18 hours at 120°F., or until crisp. Cool. Test by cutting through center to be sure there is no moisture. Celery is especially susceptible to mold unless it is perfectly dry to the center. While drying, stir slices occasionally and rotate trays once or twice.

Sun: Spread slices sparsely over trays and place in full sun where there is good air circulation. Dry 2 to 3 days, taking inside at night and stirring well occasionally. Test for moisture before storing.

Oven or Homemade Dryer: Spread a thin layer of slices over trays. Dry at 120°F. until crisp, 18 to 24 hours. Stir slices and rotate trays occasionally during drying.

To Use: Drop slices into simmering soup stock and cook with the soup. To use as a vegetable, pour 1 cup boiling water over 1 cup dried celery and simmer 20 to 30 minutes in a covered saucepan. One cup will yield about 1½ cups cooked celery.

DRIED CELERY AU GRATIN

1½ cups boiling water	1 cup milk
1½ cups dried celery slices	½ teaspoon salt
2 tablespoons butter or margarine	¾ cup American cheese, shredded
3 tablespoons all-purpose flour	

Pour boiling water over celery in a saucepan. Cover and cook 20 to 30 minutes until tender. Drain, reserving liquid. In another pan, melt butter or margarine. Stir in flour and blend well. Gradually add milk, stirring constantly. Add salt and cheese. Cook over low heat, stirring constantly until smooth and thickened. Arrange alternate layers of celery and cheese sauce in casserole. Top with a layer of cheese sauce. Bake in 350°F. oven 20 minutes until lightly browned. Serves 6.

DRIED CELERY
AND GREEN BEANS

½ cup boiling water	½ teaspoon salt
½ cup dried celery	1 tablespoon butter or margarine
2 cups cooked or canned green beans	

Pour boiling water over celery. Cover and cook 20 to 30 minutes until tender. Add remaining ingredients and cook 20 minutes longer. Serves 6.

CORN

Husk and trim sweet, immature ears of corn. Steam or water blanch until kernels are no longer milky, 1½ to 3 minutes. Drain without cooling. Cut kernels from cob.

Dehydrator: Spread kernels over trays. Dry at 120°F., stirring corn and rotating trays every 4 hours. Dry 8 to 12 hours until kernels are shriveled and dry inside.

Sun: Spread kernels over cheesecloth-covered trays and dry 1 to 2 days in full sun, stirring occasionally and taking trays inside at night. When dry, corn should be hard and brittle and should rattle in the storage jar.

Oven or Homemade Dryer: Spread kernels in a thin layer over trays. Dry at 120°F., stirring occasionally and rotating trays once or twice until corn is hard and brittle, 12 to 18 hours.

To Use: Pour 2 cups boiling water over 1 cup corn and simmer, covered, about 50 minutes until corn is tender. One cup yields approximately 2 cups cooked corn.

SCALLOPED DRIED CORN

3 cups boiling water
1½ cups dried corn
2 teaspoons chopped, dried pimiento
4 tablespoons butter or margarine
2 tablespoons all-purpose flour

½ teaspoon salt
Dash pepper
2 eggs, beaten
½ cup dried bread crumbs
Paprika

Pour boiling water over dried corn and pimiento in a saucepan. Cover and cook over low heat until tender, about 50 minutes. Drain, reserving liquid in a measuring cup. Add water to liquid to make 1 cup. In another pan, melt 2 tablespoons butter or margarine and blend in flour. Gradually stir in 1 cup cooking liquid. Cook over low heat, stirring constantly, until thickened. Season with salt and pepper. Remove from heat and add eggs, stirring constantly. Mix in drained corn and pimiento. Pour into greased casserole. Melt remaining 2 tablespoons butter or margarine and stir in dried bread crumbs. Sprinkle over top of casserole. Add a sprinkling of paprika. Set in a shallow pan of water and bake in a 350°F. oven 45 to 50 minutes. Serves 4 to 6.

DRIED CORN FRITTERS

1 cup boiling water
1 cup dried corn
1 cup all-purpose flour
½ teaspoon salt
1 teaspoon baking powder

2 eggs
¼ cup milk
1 tablespoon butter or margarine, melted
Hot oil for frying

Pour boiling water over dried corn in a saucepan. Cover and cook 40 to 50 minutes until tender. Drain. Combine flour, salt, and baking powder in a bowl. Mix eggs with milk and add melted butter or margarine and corn. Combine two mixtures lightly. Drop by teaspoonfuls into deep, hot oil. Fry until golden and cooked to center, 4 to 5 minutes. Drain on paper toweling. Serves 4 to 6.

CUCUMBERS

Wash slender, dark green cucumbers in which seeds have not yet developed. Slice, without peeling, into ⅛-inch slices.

Dehydrator: Spread slices in a single layer over trays without overlapping. Dry at 120°F. 4 to 5 hours. Turn slices and rotate trays. Continue drying another 5 to 6 hours, or until slices are crisp enough to snap in half.

Sun: Spread slices on trays and place in full sun where there is good air circulation. Dry 2 to 3 days, turning slices every day and taking trays inside at night. Dry until very brittle.

Oven or Homemade Dryer: Spread cucumber slices in a single layer over trays. Dry at 120°F. until crisp, turning occasionally and rotating trays once or twice. Will dry in 12 to 18 hours.

To Use: Eat crisp slices as a snack, with or without a cheese dip. Break or cut into pieces and add to salads just before serving. Dried cucumbers have an excellent flavor and texture and are best eaten when dry because they tend to become limp when refreshed.

EGGPLANT

Cut whole eggplant into ¼-inch slices. Peel slices. Leave slices whole, cut into ½-inch strips or in 1-inch squares. Steam blanch 4 minutes for larger pieces, 3 minutes for smaller pieces. Do not water blanch.

Dehydrator: Spread slices or pieces over trays. Dry at 120°F. 18 to 24 hours, or until leathery with no moisture in the center. Turn slices or stir pieces occasionally and rotate trays once or twice.

Sun: Spread slices or pieces over drying trays without overlapping. Dry in full sun in an area with good air circulation 2 to 3 days, until dry and leathery. Turn slices or stir pieces occasionally during drying and take trays inside at night.

Oven or Homemade Dryer: Spread slices or pieces over drying trays. Dry at 120°F. 24 to 36 hours, stirring or turning every few hours and rotating trays 2 or 3 times.

To Use: Refresh slices by soaking 3 to 4 hours or overnight in the refrigerator. Prepare as you would fresh eggplant slices by frying or in casseroles. Pieces may be soaked 1 to 2 hours before cooking or may be cooked without soaking. One cup yields about 1¼ cups cooked eggplant.

DRIED EGGPLANT CASSEROLE

12 dried eggplant slices	½ pound Mozzarella cheese, sliced
2 cups boiling water	3 tomatoes, sliced
1 egg, beaten	½ teaspoon dried oregano
⅓ cup milk	1 tablespoon olive oil
¼ teaspoon salt	
3 tablespoons cooking oil, heated in skillet	

Soak eggplant slices in boiling water 3 to 4 hours or overnight in refrigerator. In a small bowl, combine egg, milk, and salt. Dip eggplant slices in egg mixture and lightly brown in skillet in 3 tablespoons cooking oil. As slices are browned, arrange in a casserole. On top of slices, place slices of cheese and tomatoes. Repeat layers, ending with cheese. Add oregano. Brush cheese with olive oil. Bake in 350°F. oven 30 minutes. Serves 6.

MARINATED DRIED EGGPLANT

Marinate dried eggplant slices in French dressing 2 to 3 hours in the refrigerator. Lift slices from dressing into a casserole. Dot with butter or margarine and bake in 400°F. oven 20 to 25 minutes.

GREEN BEANS

Pick green beans while still immature, before beans have developed inside the pods. Wash and trim. Cut French-style (lengthwise), snap in half, or leave whole. Steam blanch 4 minutes or water blanch 2 minutes. Do not chill in cold water. Drain.

Dehydrator: Spread beans in a single layer over trays. Dry at 120°F. stirring once or twice and rotating trays. Dry 8 to 14 hours, until leathery and greenish black in color. Whole beans will take much longer to dry than cut beans.

Sun: Spread cut or whole beans on trays and place in a well-ventilated place in full sun.Dry, stirring occasionally, until leathery and dark colored, 2 to 3 days. Take inside at night.

Oven or Homemade Dryer: Spread cut or whole beans over trays in a thin layer. Dry at 120°F. 18 to 24 hours, until leathery and dark colored. Stir occasionally and rotate trays once or twice.

To Use: Pour 2 cups boiling water over 1 cup beans. Cover and simmer over low heat until beans are plump and tender, about 45 minutes. One cup yields about 2½ cups cooked beans.

DRIED GREEN BEANS
TARRAGON

2 cups boiling water	4 slices bacon, diced
¾ cup dried green beans	½ teaspoon salt
2 tablespoons dried onion, minced	1 tablespoon tarragon vinegar

Pour boiling water over dried green beans and onion in saucepan. Cover and cook over low heat 45 minutes until plump and tender. Meanwhile, sauté diced bacon in a small skillet until brown. Add bacon and seasonings to cooked green beans. Mix lightly and serve. Serves 4 to 6.

DRIED GREEN BEANS IN
MUSTARD SAUCE

2 cups boiling water

1 cup dried green beans, cut French style

2 tablespoons dried onion, minced

1 tablespoon prepared mustard

2½ teaspoons all-purpose flour

½ teaspoon salt

1 egg yolk

¾ cup milk

1 tablespoon lemon juice

Pour hot water over dried green beans in a saucepan. Add onion, cover, and cook over low heat 45 minutes until tender. Drain. Meanwhile, combine mustard, flour and salt in a pan over hot water. In a bowl, combine beaten egg yolk and milk. Add gradually to mustard mixture, stirring well. Cook until thickened, stirring constantly. Add lemon juice and pour over drained, cooked green beans. Serves 4 to 6.

GREEN TOMATOES

Pick medium-sized tomatoes while still green and firm, before they begin to ripen inside. Trim off core and blossom end and cut in ¼-inch slices.

Dehydrator: Spread slices over dehydrator trays with the slices touching but not overlapping. Dry 6 to 8 hours at 120°F. Turn slices and rotate trays. Dry another 6 to 8 hours. Cool a few slices and test for dryness. When dry, slices will be crisp, brittle and almost transparent.

Sun: Spread slices in a single layer on cheesecloth-covered trays. Dry in an area with good air circulation in hot sun, turning slices occasionally and taking trays inside at night. Slices will dry in 2 to 3 days of dry weather.

Oven or Homemade Dryer: Spread slices in a single layer over trays. Dry at 120°F. until crisp and transparent looking, 18 to 24 hours. Turn slices and rotate trays once or twice during drying.

To Use: To refresh slices, spread out on a large plate or platter. Spray with warm water and let set 30 minutes, spraying occasionally. Dip in flour and sauté in butter or margarine or use in cooking as you would fresh green tomatoes.

ITALIAN GREEN TOMATOES

12 green tomato slices	¼ pound process cheese, grated
Warm water	2 tablespoons oil
1 egg, beaten	4 tablespoons onion, minced
3 tablespoons flour	1 cup tomato sauce
½ teaspoon salt	½ teaspoon sugar
6 tablespoons cooking oil, heated for frying	¼ teaspoon salt
	¼ teaspoon dried oregano

Spray dried tomato slices with warm water. Soak 30 minutes, spraying or sprinkling with water occasionally. Dip refreshed green tomato slices in beaten egg, then in flour to which salt has been added. Sauté quickly in hot oil until golden brown. As they are browned, arrange layers of green tomato slices in a casserole alternately with grated cheese. When all slices are browned, wipe out skillet with a paper towel and add oil. Heat slowly, then sauté minced onion over low heat until transparent but not browned. Add tomato sauce, sugar, salt and oregano. Simmer 5 minutes. Pour over green tomatoes and cheese in casserole. Bake in 350°F. oven 20 to 25 minutes or until cheese is melted. Serves 4 to 6.

DRIED GREEN TOMATOES
AND OKRA

2 cups boiling water	12 dried okra pods, sliced
12 dried green tomato slices	Salt and pepper to taste
½ cup dried onion, sliced or chopped	2 tablespoons butter or margarine
1 cup dried ripe tomatoes	1 teaspoon dried parsley leaves

Pour boiling water over green tomato slices. Combine in a saucepan with dried onion, dried tomatoes and dried okra. Simmer 30 minutes. Season with salt and pepper and butter or margarine. Sprinkle with parsley. Serves 4 to 6.

GREENS (beet tops, collards, kale, mustard greens, spinach, Swiss chard)

Trim and wash greens through several waters. Steam blanch 3 minutes or water blanch 1½ minutes, until leaves go limp. Drain well. Chop leaves.

Dehydrator: Spread greens in a thin layer over trays and dry 12 to 18 hours at 120°F. until crisp. Stir once or twice during drying and rotate trays once.

Sun: Spread greens in a thin layer over cheesecloth-covered trays. Dry in a well-ventilated area in full sun, taking trays in at night and stirring several times during the day. Leaves should be very crisp when dried. Takes 1 or 2 days.

Oven or Homemade Dryer: Spread blanched greens thinly over trays. Dry at 120°F. Stir occasionally and rotate trays once or twice a day. Greens should be crisp in 18 to 24 hours.

To Use: Pour 1½ cups boiling water over 3 cups greens. Cover and cook 15 minutes over low heat. Dried greens also may be crumbled and dropped into simmering soup broth and cooked to desired tenderness. A delicious cream of spinach soup may be made by crumbling dried spinach (or any greens) into a cooked thin white sauce. Stir well, then let set 30 minutes. Stir well again and reheat.

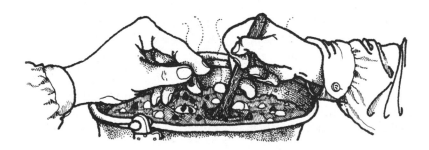

Clear soup broths may be given a delicious flavor and valuable nutrition by adding 2 teaspoons dried spinach powder, made by crushing dried spinach (or other greens) with a rolling pin or processing in the blender. Three cups yields 1½ cups cooked vegetable.

DRIED GREENS
WITH BACON DRESSING

1½ cups boiling water
3 cups dried greens
2 tablespoons dried green onions, chopped
4 slices bacon

2 tablespoons vinegar
½ teaspoon dry mustard
1½ teaspoons sugar
Salt and pepper to taste
2 hard-cooked eggs, sliced

Pour boiling water over dried greens and onions in a saucepan. Cover and cook 15 minutes, until greens are tender. Drain and put in a serving dish. Fry bacon until crisp. Remove bacon to drain on paper towels. To bacon fat in skillet, add vinegar, mustard, sugar, salt and pepper to taste. Stir well. Pour over spinach in serving dish. Top with egg slices and bacon, crumbled. Serves 4.

CREAMED DRIED GREENS

1½ cups boiling water
3 cups dried greens
2 tablespoons butter or margarine
1½ tablespoons all-purpose flour
Dash nutmeg
½ cup milk

1 chicken-flavored bouillon cube or 1 teaspoon chicken-flavored broth granules
½ teaspoon dried onion, minced
Salt and pepper

Pour boiling water over dried greens in saucepan. Cover and cook 15 minutes, until tender. Drain, reserving cooking liquid for soups. In another pan, melt butter or margarine. Stir in flour and nutmeg and gradually stir in milk. Add bouillon, onion, and salt and pepper to taste. Cook, stirring constantly, until smooth and thickened. Add to hot, drained greens. Serves 4.

KOHLRABI

Remove leaves from medium kohlrabi bulbs. Peel bulbs and cut into small cubes or thin slices. Blanch in boiling water 2 to 3 minutes or in steam 3 to 4 minutes. Drain but do not cool in cold water.

Dehydrator: Spread pieces or slices in a thin layer over trays. Dry at 120°F. 18 to 24 hours, until crisp and dry to center. Stir pieces or turn slices and rotate trays at least once during drying.

Sun: Spread pieces or slices thinly over trays and place in full sun in a well-ventilated area. Dry 2 to 3 days, until crisp and thoroughly dry, taking inside at night and stirring occasionally.

Oven or Homemade Dryer: Spread pieces or slices in a thin layer over trays. Dry at 120°F. 24 to 36 hours, until crisp, stirring occasionally and rotating trays front to back, side to side, and top to bottom once or twice.

To Use: Pour 3 cups boiling water over 1 cup vegetable pieces or slices. Cover and cook 30 to 45 minutes until tender. Serve hot, seasoned with butter or margarine and salt and pepper. Garnish with broiled mushrooms or grated nutmeats. One cup dried yields about 1½ cups cooked vegetable.

DRIED KOHLRABI AU GRATIN

4½ cups boiling water	Salt and pepper
1½ cups dried kohlrabi slices	2 tablespoons butter or margarine
3 tablespoons butter or margarine	½ cup dried bread crumbs
3 tablespoons all-purpose flour	½ cup cheddar cheese, grated
1½ cups milk	

Pour boiling water over dried kohlrabi slices in a saucepan. Cover and cook over low heat 30 to 45 minutes, until tender. Drain, reserving liquid for soups. Place one-half of cooked kohlrabi in a casserole. In a saucepan,

110

melt 3 tablespoons butter or margarine and blend in flour. Gradually add milk and cook, stirring constantly, until smooth and thickened. Season to taste with salt and pepper. Pour one half of sauce over kohlrabi slices in casserole; add remaining cooked slices, then rest of sauce. Top with bread crumbs which have been mixed with 2 tablespoons melted butter or margarine and grated cheddar cheese. Bake in 350°F. oven 30 minutes, until bubbly hot and lightly browned. Serves 6.

DRIED KOHLRABI
PATTIES

4½ cups boiling water

1½ cups dried kohlrabi pieces

2 tablespoons butter or margarine

Salt and pepper

3 tablespoons all-purpose flour

3 tablespoons cooking oil, heated for frying

Pour boiling water over dried pieces. Cook 30 to 35 minutes in a covered saucepan, until tender. Drain and mash with a fork or potato masher. Season with 2 tablespoons butter or margarine and salt and pepper to taste. Form into small patties and dip in flour. Brown in hot oil. Serves 4.

LETTUCE

Trim coarse outer leaves and hearts from lettuce heads. Shred or cut into quarters. Blanch until wilted, 2 to 2½ minutes in steam or 1½ minutes in boiling water. Drain, but do not chill.

Dehydrator: Spread shreds or quarters thinly over trays. Dry at 120°F. until crisp, 8 to 12 hours, stirring or turning pieces occasionally and rotating trays once. When dry, a cooled piece should crumble easily when crushed in the hands.

Sun: Spread shreds or place quarters on drying trays in full sun. Dry 2 to 3 days in a well-ventilated place until crisp, taking trays inside at night and stirring pieces occasionally. To test for dryness, cool a piece, then crush in the hand. It should crumble easily.

Oven or Homemade Dryer: Spread shreds or quarters thinly over trays. Dry at 120°F. until crisp, 6 to 8 hours. Stir occasionally and rotate trays once or twice a day.

To Use: While refreshed lettuce does not have the crispness desirable for salads, it is an excellent cooked vegetable and a valuable addition to soups. Pour one cup boiling water over 1 cup dried lettuce, cover and cook over low heat 20 minutes. Season to taste with butter or margarine, salt and pepper. Or drop shreds of dried lettuce into simmering soup and cook 20 to 25 minutes. One cup yields about 1½ cups cooked vegetable.

BRAISED
DRIED LETTUCE

4 dried lettuce quarters	Salt and pepper
2 cups boiling water	Dash of nutmeg
2 tablespoons butter or margarine	1 tablespoon lemon juice

Cook dried lettuce quarters in boiling water 30 to 35 minutes. Drain, reserving liquid for soups. Melt butter or margarine in a heavy skillet. Add lettuce and cook slowly 10 to 15 minutes. Add seasoning and lemon juice and stir quickly to blend. Serves 4.

SWEET AND SOUR
DRIED LETTUCE

3 cups dried lettuce shreds	2 tablespoons all-purpose flour
1 cup dried apple slices	3 tablespoons vinegar
4 cups boiling water	4 tablespoons brown sugar
2 tablespoons cooking oil	Salt and pepper

Cover dried lettuce and dried apple slices with boiling water. Cook 10 minutes in a covered saucepan. Add oil and cook another 10 to 15 minutes. Sprinkle with flour, vinegar, and sugar. Mix well. Season to taste with salt and pepper. Simmer 5 minutes more. Serves 6.

MUSHROOMS

Select only commercially grown varieties or those that you know beyond any doubt are non-toxic. The toxins of poisonous mushrooms are not destroyed by the drying or cooking processes. Wash mushrooms quickly in cold water without soaking or peeling. Trim ⅛ inch off the stem end. Slice thinly or chop fine. Do not blanch.

Dehydrator: Spread slices or pieces thinly over trays. Dry at 120°F. for 8 to 12 hours, stirring occasionally and rotating trays once or twice. Well-dried mushrooms should be tough and leathery, with no sign of moisture in the center when cut.

Sun: Spread slices or pieces over trays and dry in full sun 1 or 2 days. Choose a drying area with good air circulation and dry until tough and leathery, with no sign of moisture in the centers.

Oven or Homemade Dryer: Spread slices or pieces in a thin layer over trays. Dry at 120°F. 12 to 18 hours, until pieces are tough and leathery, stirring occasionally and rotating trays once or twice.

To Use: Pour 1 cup boiling water over 1 cup mushrooms. Cook in a covered saucepan 20 to 30 minutes, until plump and tender. One cup will yield about 1¼ cups cooked mushrooms.

DRIED MUSHROOMS BAKED IN CREAM

1 cup boiling water	2 tablespoons all-purpose flour
1 cup dried mushrooms	1 cup milk
2 tablespoons butter or margarine	Salt and pepper

Pour boiling water over dried mushrooms in a saucepan. Cook 20 to 30 minutes, until tender. Drain, reserving any liquid for use in soups. Place mushrooms in a 1-quart casserole. Melt butter or margarine in saucepan. Blend in flour and gradually add milk. Cook, stirring constantly until smooth and thickened. Season to taste with salt and pepper. Pour sauce over mushrooms in casserole and bake in 350°F. oven 30 to 35 minutes. Serve over hot toast. Serves 4.

DRIED MUSHROOM CROQUETTES

¾ cup dried mushrooms
¾ cup boiling water
1 tablespoon butter or margarine
1 tablespoon all-purpose flour
½ cup milk
½ teaspoon Worcestershire sauce
⅛ teaspoon curry powder

1 egg
2 tablespoons dried bread crumbs
½ teaspoon salt
½ cup dried bread crumbs
Deep cooking oil for frying, heated to 360°F.

Cook dried mushrooms in boiling water 20 to 30 minutes. Drain, reserving any liquid for soups. In a saucepan, melt butter or margarine and blend in flour. Gradually add milk and cook, stirring constantly, until smooth and thickened. To this sauce add mushrooms, Worcestershire sauce, curry powder, egg, 2 tablespoons bread crumbs, and salt. Shape into croquettes and chill thoroughly. Roll in ½ cup fine bread crumbs and fry until golden brown in deep, hot cooking oil. Serves 4 to 6.

OKRA

Select young, tender, 2-to 4-inch okra pods which snap easily. Wash well and cut off stem ends. Cut crosswise in ¼-inch slices. Blanching is not necessary.

Dehydrator: Spread slices in a thin layer over trays. Dry 8 to 12 hours at 120°F. until very brittle. Stir slices and rotate trays after 4 or 5 hours.

Sun: Spread slices in a thin layer over trays. Dry in hot sun in a well-ventilated place 1 or 2 days, taking trays inside at night and stirring slices occasionally. Slices should be brittle when dry.

Oven or Homemade Dryer: Spread slices thinly over trays. Dry at 120°F. 12 to 18 hours, until brittle, stirring occasionally and rotating trays once or twice.

To Use: Cook slices 30 to 45 minutes, using 2 cups boiling water to each cup dried okra. One cup will yield 1½ cups cooked vegetable.

BAKED
DRIED OKRA

3 cups boiling water
1½ cups dried okra slices
¼ cup dried onion slices

2 tablespoons butter or margarine, melted
Salt and pepper
1 cup tomato sauce

Pour boiling water over okra and onion slices in a 1½-quart casserole. Let soak 3 to 4 hours. Drain. Season with butter or margarine and salt and pepper to taste. Top with tomato sauce and bake 30 to 45 minutes in a 350° F. oven. Serves 4 to 6.

STEWED DRIED OKRA
AND RICE

3 cups boiling water
1 cup dried okra slices
1 cup dried tomatoes
¼ cup dried onion, chopped

2 tablespoons cooking oil
3 tablespoons uncooked rice (not Minute rice)
½ teaspoon salt

Combine all ingredients in a medium-sized saucepan. Cover and cook over low heat 30 to 45 minutes, until rice is cooked and vegetables are tender. Stir occasionally to keep from sticking. Serves 4 to 6.

ONIONS

Although onions keep well for several months when air-cured 2 to 3 weeks after harvest, chopped, dried onions are a convenience to keep as a quick seasoning on the kitchen shelf or at the vacation cabin. Sliced, dried onions are a must for backpackers or anyone who plans to cook meals outdoors. In the spring, when winter-stored onions threaten to sprout, they may be saved by slicing or chopping them and drying them for later use. Peel and cut onions in ⅛-inch slices or chop fine. No blanching is needed.

Dehydrator: Spread sliced or chopped onions over trays. Dry at 120°F. until brittle, 12 to 24 hours, stirring pieces or turning slices after the first 8 hours, and rotating trays once or twice.

Sun: Spread chopped or sliced onions evenly over trays and dry in full sun in a well-ventilated place until papery and brittle, 2 to 3 days. Take trays inside at night and stir pieces or turn slices occasionally during drying.

Oven or Homemade Dryer: Spread slices or pieces in a thin layer over trays. Dry at 120°F., 24 to 36 hours until brittle, stirring occasionally and rotating trays once or twice.

To Use: They may be used as seasoning in soups, salads, or cooked dishes without refreshing. Simply measure one-half as much dried onion as the fresh onion called for in the recipe. To refresh dried onions, soak 45 minutes using 2 cups boiling water to every cup dried onion. One cup will yield about 1⅓ cups refreshed onion.

CREAMED
DRIED ONIONS

2 cups boiling water	½ teaspoon salt
1 cup dried onion slices	½ cup dried onion slices
¼ cup dried mushroom slices	2 tablespoons butter or margarine, melted
2 tablespoons butter or margarine	
2 tablespoons flour	2 tablespoons dried cheese, grated
1 cup milk	

Pour boiling water over 1 cup onion slices and mushroom slices. Soak 45 minutes. Meanwhile, melt 2 tablespoons butter or margarine in a saucepan. Blend in flour and gradually add milk. Add salt. Cook, stirring constantly, until smooth and thickened. Add drained onion and mushroom slices and pour them into a casserole. Melt remaining 2 tablespoons butter or margarine and add ½ cup dried onion slices (not soaked) and dried, grated cheese. Sprinkle over top of casserole. Bake in 350°F. oven until bubbly hot and lightly browned, 20 to 25 minutes. Serves 6.

DRIED ONION PIE

3 cups boiling water

1½ cups dried onion slices

1 cup all-purpose flour

¼ teaspoon salt

⅓ cup shortening

¼ cup (about) ice water

6 slices bacon

2 eggs, beaten

1 egg yolk

¾ cup sour cream

Salt and pepper

⅛ teaspoon caraway seed

½ teaspoon dried chopped chives

Paprika

Pour boiling water over dried onion slices. Soak 45 minutes. Add salt to flour. Using a pastry blender or two knives, cut the shortening into the flour until it is the consistency of coarse meal. Add enough ice water to make a stiff dough. Roll out to the size of a 9-inch pie pan, making a fluted edge around the rim. Chill.

Fry bacon until crisp. Remove and drain on paper toweling. Pour off all but 3 tablespoons bacon fat. Cook refreshed onion slices in fat until yellow but not browned, stirring often. Crumble bacon into large pieces and add to the onion. Add eggs, sour cream, salt, pepper, caraway seed, and chives. Pour into chilled, unbaked pie shell. Sprinkle with paprika. Bake in a 425°F. oven 10 minutes. Reduce heat to 350°F. and bake another 25 to 30 minutes until set in the center. Serve hot. Serves 6 to 8.

PARSNIPS

Scrape or peel parsnips, trimming off root and top ends. Cut in ⅛-inch slices or chop in small pieces. Blanching is not necessary for eating dry, but parsnips to be used for cooking should be blanched 3 minutes in water, 4 minutes in steam.

Dehydrator: Spread slices or pieces thinly over trays. Dry 8 to 12 hours at 120°F. until crisp, turning slices or stirring pieces occasionally. Rotate trays at least once.

Sun: Spread slices or pieces in a thin layer over trays and place in hot sun in a well-ventilated area. Dry 2 to 3 days, taking inside at night and stirring once or twice a day. Dry until brittle.

Oven or Homemade Dryer: Spread slices or pieces evenly over trays. Dry at 120°F. until crisp, 12 to 18 hours, stirring occasionally and rotating trays once or twice.

To Use: The slices are delicious eaten as a snack alone or with a cheese dip. To cook slices or chopped pieces, pour 2 cups boiling water over 1 cup dried parsnips. Cover and simmer until tender, 30 to 45 minutes. One cup yields about 1½ cups cooked vegetable.

MASHED DRIED PARSNIPS

3 cups boiling water
1½ cups dried parsnips
3 tablespoons butter or margarine

½ cup hot milk
Salt and pepper

Pour boiling water over parsnips in a saucepan. Cover and cook over low heat 30 to 45 minutes, until tender. Drain well. Mash with a potato masher or electric mixer. Add butter or margarine and beat until melted. Gradually add hot milk, mixing until milk is absorbed and parsnips are fluffy. Season to taste with salt and pepper. Serves 4 to 6.

DRIED PARSNIPS
CONTINENTAL

4 cups boiling water
2 cups dried parsnips
¼ cup butter or margarine, melted
1 teaspoon sugar

½ teaspoon salt
3 tablespoons lemon juice
1 cup sour cream

Pour boiling water over dried parsnips in saucepan. Cover and cook until tender, 30 to 45 minutes. Drain. In a bowl combine melted butter or margarine, sugar, salt, lemon juice and sour cream. Pour into a casserole. Pour cooked parsnips over sauce and bake in 350°F. oven 20 to 25 minutes. Serves 6.

PEAS

Shell immature green peas within a few hours of picking. Steam blanch 3 minutes or blanch in boiling water 2 minutes. Drain without cooling.

Dehydrator: Spread blanched peas in a thin layer over trays. Dry 12 to 18 hours at 120°F. until wrinkled and hard. Well-dried peas will split in two when tapped with a hammer. Stir occasionally and rotate trays once or twice.

Sun: Spread blanched peas over trays and place in full sun in a well-ventilated area. Dry 2 to 3 days until wrinkled and hard enough to split when tapped with a hammer. Take trays inside at night and stir occasionally during drying.

Oven or Homemade Dryer: Spread blanched peas in a thin layer over trays. Dry at 120° F. until hard and brittle, 18 to 24 hours. Stir peas occasionally and rotate trays once or twice.

To Use: Pour 2 cups boiling water over 1 cup peas and cook 40 to 45 minutes in a covered saucepan. One cup will yield about 2 cups cooked peas.

PUREE OF
GREEN PEA SOUP

2 cups boiling water

1 cup dried peas

½ teaspoon salt

2 tablespoons butter or margarine

½ cup cream or top milk

Pour boiling water over dried peas. Cover and cook until tender, 40 to 45 minutes. Add salt. Put peas and cooking water through a food strainer, food mill, or electric blender. Add butter or margarine and cream. Reheat to simmering. Serves 4 to 6.

BUTTERED DRIED PEAS
AND ONIONS

1½ cups boiling water	1 tablespoon dried onion, minced
¾ cup dried peas	½ cup boiling water
¼ teaspoon salt	¼ cup butter or margarine
2 tablespoons dried mushroom slices	12 small pearl onions, cooked

Pour boiling water over dried peas in a saucepan. Cover and cook 40 to 45 minutes. Drain and add salt. Meanwhile, combine dried mushrooms and 1 tablespoon dried onion in a bowl. Cover with boiling water and soak 15 to 20 minutes. Drain. Melt butter or margarine in a small skillet and add drained, refreshed mushrooms and onion. Stir-fry until golden over low heat. Combine cooked peas and hot, cooked pearl onions in a serving dish and top with sautéd mushrooms and onions. Serves 4 to 6.

PEAS (black-eyed peas, cow peas, crowder peas, chick peas)

Allow peas to ripen completely and dry as much as possible on the vine. Shell. No blanching is necessary.

Dehydrator: Spread partially dried peas in a single layer over trays. Dry at 120°F., stirring occasionally, until a cooled dried pea will split when tapped with a hammer, 8 to 10 hours depending on the stage of dryness at which they were picked. Rotate trays once during drying.

Sun: Spread partially dried peas in a thin layer over drying trays and place in a well-ventilated spot in full sun. Dry 2 or 3 days, until peas will split when tapped with a hammer. Stir occasionally and take trays inside at night.

Oven or Homemade Dryer: Spread partially dried peas thinly over drying trays. Dry at 120°F. until peas are hard and brittle, 12 to 15 hours.

To Use: Soak peas in water to cover 3 or 4 hours, or overnight. Drain, add fresh water and cook over low heat 2 to 3 hours until tender. One cup will yield about 2 cups cooked peas.

SAVORY DRIED PEAS

4 cups boiling water

2 cups dried peas (black-eyed peas, cow peas, crowder peas, or chick peas)

1 teaspoon salt

¼ teaspoon pepper

2 ounces sliced salt pork

4 small onions, peeled

Pour boiling water over peas. Soak 3 to 4 hours. Drain. Add fresh water to cover, salt, pepper, pork, and onions. Cover and cook over low heat until tender, about 1 hour. Serves 4 to 6.

SPANISH DRIED PEAS

2 cups boiling water

1 cup dried peas (black-eyed peas, cow peas, crowder peas, or chick peas)

1 slice salt pork or ham

1 large onion, sliced

1 mild chili pepper, sliced

2 tomatoes or 1 cup canned tomatoes

1 bouquet garni (see herb section)

3 quarts cold water

Bones from 1 or 2 roasted or fried chickens

Salt and pepper to taste

½ teaspoon dried mint, crumbled

Pour boiling water over dried peas. Let soak 3 to 4 hours. Drain. Put in kettle with salt pork or ham, onion, chili pepper, tomatoes, bouquet garni, water, and chicken bones. Cover and simmer until peas are tender, 1 to 2 hours. Remove chicken bones and bouquet garni. Put vegetables and broth through a sieve, food mill, or electric blender. Add salt and pepper to taste. Add mint. Reheat and serve piping hot. Serves 6.

PEPPERS–PIMIENTOS
(see herb section for other peppers)

Wash, stem, and core thick-walled green or ripe bell peppers or red-ripe pimientos. Remove all inner white membrane. Cut in halves, into thin crosswise slices, lengthwise strips, or coarsely chop. Blanching is not necessary.

Dehydrator: Spread halves, slices or pieces in a thin layer over trays. Dry at 120°F. until leathery, 12 to 18 hours for halves, 8 to 12 hours for slices and pieces. Stir occasionally or turn halves. Rotate trays once or twice during drying.

Sun: Spread halves, slices or pieces thinly over trays. Place trays in full sun in an area with good air circulation. Dry halves 2 to 3 days, slices and pieces 1 to 2 days, until leathery and completely dry. Turn halves and stir pieces occasionally and take trays inside at night.

Oven or Homemade Dryer: Spread slices or pieces over trays. Dry at 120°F. 18 to 24 hours, until leathery with no moisture inside, stirring occasionally and rotating trays once. Halves do not dry well in the oven.

To Use: Slices and chopped pieces may be used in soups, casseroles, meat loaves, and salads in dry form, without refreshing. For each 3 tablespoons fresh green pepper or pimiento called for in a recipe, 2 tablespoons dried pepper may be substituted. Green pepper or pimiento halves may be refreshed by soaking in boiling water to cover 30 to 45 minutes. Use as you would fresh peppers.

CHEESE-STUFFED
DRIED GREEN PEPPERS

2 cups boiling water
6 dried green pepper halves (or pimientos)
2 cups cooked rice
½ cup milk
1 tablespoon dried pimiento, chopped

1 tablespoon dried parsley, chopped
1 tablespoon dried onion, chopped
½ teaspoon salt
⅛ teaspoon pepper
2 tablespoons butter or margarine, melted
1 cup cheddar cheese, grated

Pour boiling water over pepper halves. Let soak 30 to 45 minutes. Simmer over low heat 10 minutes. Drain. Combine cooked rice, milk, dried pimiento, parsley, onion, salt and pepper, melted butter or margarine, and grated cheese. Pile into green pepper halves. Place peppers in a baking pan into which one-half cup water has been poured. Bake in 350°F. oven 30 minutes. Serves 6.

SALMON-STUFFED
DRIED PIMIENTOS

2 cups boiling water	¾ cup milk
12 dried pimiento halves	1 egg, beaten
1 (1-pound) can salmon	2 teaspoons lemon juice
2 tablespoons dried onion	¼ cup dried bread crumbs
½ cup dried bread crumbs	2 tablespoons dried cheese, grated

Pour boiling water over dried pimiento halves. Let soak 30 minutes. Cover and simmer 10 minutes. Drain. Combine salmon, onion, ½ cup bread crumbs, milk, egg, and lemon juice. Pile onto pimiento halves. Top with ¼ cup bread crumbs which have been mixed with grated cheese. Set in baking pan containing ½ cup hot water. Bake in 350°F. oven 15 to 20 minutes. Serves 6.

POTATOES

Dried potatoes are convenient for camping and hiking trips or wherever weight is a consideration. They must be watched carefully, however, for any hint of moisture will cause the entire batch to mold. Wash and peel potatoes and cut into ¼-inch shoestring strips or ⅛-inch slices. Blanch in steam 6 to 8 minutes or 5 to 6 minutes in boiling water. Drain well.

Dehydrator: Spread strips or slices in a single layer over trays. Dry 12 to 18 hours at 120°F. until brittle and semi-transparent. Turn pieces and rotate trays once or twice during drying.

Sun: Spread strips or slices in a single layer over trays. Dry in a well-ventilated place in hot sun 2 to 3 days, until brittle and semi-transparent. Turn pieces occasionally and take trays inside at night.

Oven or Homemade Dryer: Spread strips or slices thinly over trays. Dry at 120°F. until brittle, turning pieces occasionally and rotating trays once or twice. Will dry in 18 to 24 hours.

123

To Use: Pour 1 cup boiling water over 1 cup potatoes. Cook 45 to 50 minutes for boiled potatoes or hash browns. One cup yields 1 to 1⅓ cups cooked potatoes.

CHEESED
DRIED POTATOES

2 cups boiling water	½ teaspoon salt
2 cups dried potato slices	1 cup milk
2 tablespoons butter or margarine	1 cup process cheese, sliced
2 tablespoons all-purpose flour	

Pour boiling water over dried potato slices. Cook 45 to 50 minutes. Drain and arrange in baking dish. In a saucepan, melt butter or margarine and blend in flour and salt. Gradually add milk and cheese. Cook, stirring constantly, until smooth and thickened. Pour over potatoes and bake in 350°F. oven 45 minutes, or until top begins to brown. Serves 6.

TOMATO-POTATO
SKILLET

3 cups boiling water	1 cup dried tomato slices
3 cups dried potatoes	1 cup water
¼ cup butter or margarine	Salt and pepper
1 cup dried onion slices	

Pour boiling water over dried potatoes. Let soak 1 to 2 hours. Drain, reserving liquid. In a heavy skillet, melt butter or margarine and add ¼ cup reserved liquid. Arrange dried potatoes, onions, and tomatoes over bottom of skillet. Add water, cover and simmer 45 to 50 minutes. Season to taste with salt and pepper. Serves 4 to 6.

PUMPKIN

Any size pumpkin may be used. Cut in half and remove seeds and core. Cut halves in ¼-inch slices. Peel each slice and cut into 1-inch pieces. Steam blanch 2½ to 3 minutes or blanch in boiling water 1½ minutes. Drain.

Or cut pumpkin halves in 1-inch slices. Peel each slice and cut into cubes. Cook until tender, 30 to 45 minutes in a steamer, 10 to 12 minutes in a pressure pan at 15 pounds pressure or 1 hour in a 325°F. oven. Cut cubes into slices. Cooked pumpkin also may be mashed with a potato masher, electric mixer or blender.

Dehydrator: Spread pieces or slices in a thin layer over trays. Dry 12 to 18 hours at 120°F. until leathery and dry to the center, rotating trays and turning pieces once or twice during drying.

To dry mashed pumpkin, spread thinly over dehydrator trays which have been covered with plastic wrap. Dry 6 to 8 hours at 120°F. until it can be pulled away from plastic. Turn pumpkin over, peel off plastic, and dry until firm and brittle. Break into pieces and reduce to a powder in an electric blender or by pounding with a pestle. Return to dehydrator for 2 hours.

Sun: Spread pieces or slices in a thin layer over trays and place in a well-ventilated area in full sun. Dry 2 to 3 days, until there is no moisture in the center and pieces are hard and brittle. Take trays inside at night and turn pieces occasionally. Process in blender to a fine powder, then return to the sun for a few more hours.

Oven or Homemade Dryer: Spread pieces over drying trays. Dry at 120°F. until hard and brittle, 18 to 24 hours, stirring occasionally and rotating trays. Process in blender to a powder, then return to oven or dryer for 2 hours.

To Use: Pour ¾ cup boiling water over ¾ cup powdered pumpkin or pumpkin pieces. Let soak 30 to 45 minutes. This will yield about 1 cup cooked puree, which may be used in puddings, pies, or in baking as you would fresh or canned pumpkin.

DRIED
PUMPKIN BREAD

1½ cups boiling water
1½ cups dried pumpkin powder
⅔ cup shortening
⅔ cup sugar
4 eggs
⅔ cup cold water
3⅓ cups all-purpose flour

2 teaspoons baking soda
1½ teaspoons salt
½ teaspoon baking powder
1 teaspoon powdered cinnamon
1 teaspoon powdered cloves
⅔ cup coarsely chopped nuts
⅔ cup chopped dried plums

Pour boiling water over dried pumpkin powder. Let soak 30 to 45 minutes. Meanwhile, in a large mixing bowl, cream shortening and sugar until fluffy. Add eggs, refreshed pumpkin and ⅔ cup cold water. Beat well. Blend in flour, soda, salt, baking powder, and spices. Stir in nuts and chopped dried plums. Pour into two 9 by 5-inch well-greased loaf pans. Bake in a 350°F. oven about 1 hour, 10 minutes, or until a toothpick inserted in the middle comes out clean.

DRIED
PUMPKIN COOKIES

1 cup boiling water
1 cup dried pumpkin powder
½ cup butter or margarine
1 cup sugar
1 egg
1 teaspoon vanilla
2 cups all-purpose flour

½ teaspoon salt
1 teaspoon baking powder
1 teaspoon baking soda
1 teaspoon powdered cinnamon
2 cups dried peaches or apricots, chopped

Pour boiling water over dried pumpkin powder. Let soak 30 to 45 minutes. Meanwhile, cream butter or margarine and sugar until fluffy. Add egg and vanilla and blend in. In another bowl, combine flour, salt, baking powder, soda, and cinnamon. Add chopped dried fruit. Add to creamed mixture, 1 cup at a time, beating well after each addition. Drop by spoonfuls onto greased cookie sheet and bake in 350°F. oven 12 to 15 minutes, until lightly browned. Yields 4 dozen cookies.

RADISHES

Wash firm, fresh, red or white radishes. Trim off root and top ends. Cut into ⅛-inch slices. Do not blanch.

Dehydrator: Spread slices sparsely over trays. Dry at 120°F. until crisp and dried through, 8 to 10 hours. Stir slices occasionally and rotate trays once.

Sun: Spread slices in a thin layer over trays and dry in hot sun 1 to 2 days, stirring occasionally and taking trays inside at night. When dry, slices will be crisp.

Oven or Homemade Dryer: Spread slices thinly over trays. Dry at 120°F., stirring occasionally and rotating trays once. Dry until crisp, 10 to 12 hours.

To Use: Eat crisp slices as a snack, alone or with a cheese dip. Add to gelatin, potato or tossed salads in dry form. To serve as a cooked vegetable, simmer about 20 minutes in an equal amount of boiling water. Season to taste with salt and butter or margarine.

RUTABAGAS

Cut off tops and roots and thinly peel rutabagas. Cut in very thin slices, dice into ⅛-inch cubes, or grate. Blanch in boiling water 3 minutes or in steam 4 minutes. Drain well. The tops may be dried as greens.

Dehydrator: Spread slices or pieces in a thin layer over trays. Dry at 120°F. until crisp, 8 to 12 hours. Stir occasionally or turn slices and rotate trays once or twice.

Sun: Spread slices or pieces over drying trays in a thin layer. Place in a well-ventilated area in full sun. Dry until crisp, 1 to 2 days, stirring occasionally and taking inside at night.

Oven or Homemade Dryer: Spread slices or pieces over drying trays in a thin layer. Dry at 120°F. until crisp, 12 to 18 hours, stirring occasionally and rotating trays once or twice.

To Use: Eat dried slices as a snack alone or with cheese dip, or chop and add in dry form to tossed salads. Chopped pieces also may be dropped into simmering soups. To cook as a vegetable, pour 1 cup boiling water over 1 cup dried rutabaga and cook 30 to 45 minutes over low heat. Mash or leave in pieces and season to taste with salt and pepper, butter or margarine. One cup will yield about 1 cup cooked vegetable.

DRIED RUTABAGA RING

2 cups boiling water	2 tablespoons brown sugar
2 cups dried rutabaga	½ teaspoon salt
3 tablespoons butter or margarine	⅛ teaspoon pepper
2 tablespoons flour	3 egg whites, stiffly beaten
½ cup milk	

Pour boiling water over dried rutabaga. Cover and cook 30 to 45 minutes, until tender. Drain. Mash with potato masher, electric mixer, or blender. In another saucepan, melt butter or margarine and blend in flour. Gradually add milk and cook over low heat, stirring constantly, until smooth and thickened. Add brown sugar, cooked rutabaga, salt and pepper. Cool. Fold stiffly beaten egg whites into rutabaga mixture. Pour into a greased 8-inch ring mold. Set in a pan of hot water and bake in 350°F. oven 45 minutes. Unmold and fill center with a hot, cooked vegetable. Serves 6.

CREAMED DRIED CARROTS
AND RUTABAGAS

2 cups boiling water
1 cup dried rutabagas
1 cup dried carrots
2 tablespoons butter or margarine
2 tablespoons all-purpose flour

1 cup milk
½ teaspoon salt
1 teaspoon chicken-flavored soup
    broth, granules or cube

Pour boiling water over dried rutabagas and carrots. Cook 45 to 50 minutes, until tender. Meanwhile, melt butter or margarine. Stir in flour. Gradually add milk. Cook over low heat, stirring constantly, until smooth and thickened. Stir in salt and chicken-flavored soup granules or cube. Stir well to dissolve. Pour over mixed carrots and rutabagas in serving dish. Serves 6.

SALSIFY

Scrub, scrape, or peel small to medium salsify roots. Cut into ⅛-inch slices. Dip in 1 quart of water to which ½ teaspoon salt or 1 tablespoon lemon juice has been added. Or blanch in boiling water 3 minutes or in a steam blancher 4 minutes. Drain well.

Dehydrator: Spread slices thinly over trays. Dry at 120°F. until crisp, 12 to 18 hours, stirring once or twice and rotating trays.

Sun: Spread slices over trays in a thin layer and place in a well-ventilated area in full sun. Dry until crisp, 1 or 2 days, stirring occasionally and taking trays inside at night, if necessary.

Oven or Homemade Dryer: Spread salsify slices thinly over drying trays. Dry at 120°F. until crisp, 18 to 24 hours, stirring slices occasionally and rotating trays once or twice.

To Use: Slices are delicious eaten as a snack or mixed with other dried vegetables. Slices are small and may be added in dried form to tossed salads. They may be grated and used as a casserole topping. Drop slices in a simmering soup and cook until tender, or cook alone by simmering in water 30 to 45 minutes. One cup yields about 1¼ cups cooked vegetable.

MOCK OYSTERS

1¾ cups boiling water
1¾ cups dried salsify
1 egg
½ teaspoon salt
⅛ teaspoon pepper

1 tablespoon butter or margarine, melted
1 egg, well beaten
Finely rolled dried bread crumbs for coating
Hot oil for frying

Pour boiling water over dried salsify in a saucepan. Cover and cook 30 to 45 minutes, until tender. Drain. Mash with a potato masher or electric mixer until fluffy. Add 1 egg, salt, pepper, and butter or margarine. Blend well. Shape into 12 oyster-sized patties. Dip in the beaten egg, then in crumbs. Fry in hot oil until golden brown on both sides. Serves 4 to 6.

DRIED SALSIFY SOUP

2 cups boiling water
1½ cups dried salsify slices
½ cup dried celery slices
6 tablespoons butter or margarine

6 tablespoons all-purpose flour
1 quart milk
Salt and pepper

Pour boiling water over dried salsify and celery slices in a saucepan. Cover and cook 30 to 45 minutes, until tender. Meanwhile, melt butter or margarine in another saucepan. Blend in flour, then gradually add milk. Cook, stirring constantly, until smooth and thickened. Add cooked salsify and celery. Season to taste with salt and pepper. Serves 4 to 6.

SAUERKRAUT

Make homemade sauerkraut by finely shredding fresh cabbage, then packing down firmly in a crock or earthenware bowl with a wooden pestle or potato masher. Sprinkle each medium head of cabbage with 2 tablespoons flaked salt. Layer cabbage and salt in crock, pressing firmly with each layer until the cabbage is covered with juice and all cabbage is used. Top with a plate which just fits the inside of the crock or bowl. Weight down with a stone or a water-filled jar so that the juice covers the plate. Cover with a clean cloth and keep at 70°F. for 2 to 3 weeks, until fermentation stops. Each day remove any film from the top and wash the plate.

Dehydrator: Drain sauerkraut well. Spread in a thin layer over trays and dry at 120°F. until crisp and dried through, 18 to 24 hours. Stir occasionally and rotate trays once or twice.

Sun: Drain sauerkraut well. Spread in a thin layer over trays which have been covered with cheesecloth. Dry in a well-ventilated area in hot sun 2 to 3 days, taking inside at night and stirring occasionally. Dry until crisp.

Oven or Homemade Dryer: Drain sauerkraut well. Spread thinly over trays and dry at 120°F. It will take 24 to 36 hours to reach the desired state of crispness.

To Use: Pour 1 cup boiling water over 1 cup sauerkraut in a saucepan. Cover and cook 45 to 50 minutes over low heat. One cup yields about 1½ cups cooked sauerkraut.

TOMATO SAUERKRAUT

2 cups boiling water	1 tablespoon all-purpose flour
2 cups dried sauerkraut	1½ cups tomato juice
¼ cup dried onion slices	1 dried bay leaf
1 tablespoon cooking oil	1 tablespoon honey

Pour boiling water over dried sauerkraut and onion slices. Set aside. In a large pan, place oil. Stir in flour and cook, stirring constantly, until lightly browned. Add sauerkraut, tomato juice, bay leaf and cover. Cook over low heat 45 to 50 minutes. Remove bay leaf and add honey. Serves 4 to 6.

DRIED SAUERKRAUT
WITH PORK

6 cups boiling water

3 cups dried sauerkraut

4 smoked pork hocks (about
  3 pounds)

1 dried bay leaf

8 peppercorns

¼ cup dried onion, chopped

1 large raw potato, grated

1 cup dried apple slices

Pour boiling water over dried sauerkraut in a large pan. Add pork hocks, bay leaf and peppercorns. Cover and simmer until tender, 2 to 3 hours. Remove meat and peppercorns. Discard peppercorns and cut meat into serving size pieces. To cooked sauerkraut add dried onion, potato and dried apple slices. Arrange cut up meat on top. Cover and simmer 30 to 45 minutes longer. Serves 6 to 8.

SPROUTS

Soybean, mung bean, alfalfa or any favorite variety of sprouts may be dried to create an entirely new-tasting vegetable. Since sprouts are at their flavorful, most nutritious best when eaten within 3 or 4 days after sprouting, it is a good idea to keep a fresh supply and dry those more than 4 days old to make use of them. As the sprouts dry, they take on a delicious, nutlike flavor. Drain well before drying. No pretreatment is necessary.

Dehydrator: Spread drained sprouts thinly over trays. Dry at 120°F. until crisp and crunchy, 8 to 12 hours. Stir occasionally and rotate trays front to back, side to side, and top to bottom once or twice.

Sun: Spread drained sprouts in a thin layer over trays and place in a well-ventilated area in full sun. Dry 1 to 2 days, stirring occasionally and taking trays inside at night, if necessary. Dry until they are crisp.

Oven or Homemade Dryer: Spread well-drained sprouts thinly over trays. Dry at 120°F. 12 to 18 hours, until crisp, stirring occasionally and rotating trays once or twice.

To Use: Try without refreshing. Add them to meat loaves, breakfast cereals and vegetables, as a topping for casseroles and to add crunch to cookies, cakes, and candies. Dried sprouts add a delicious crispness to tossed salads and scrambled eggs.

TUNA-MUSHROOM
CASSEROLE

¾ cup boiling water

¾ cup dried mushrooms

4 tablespoons butter or margarine

4 tablespoons all-purpose flour

2¼ cups milk

Salt and pepper

1 (13-ounce) can tuna, drained
and flaked

2 cups dried sprouts

Pour boiling water over dried mushrooms. Cover and simmer 30 to 45 minutes. Meanwhile, melt butter or margarine in a saucepan. Stir in flour and gradually add milk and salt and pepper to taste. Cook over low heat, stirring constantly, until smooth and thickened. Combine tuna, 1 cup dried sprouts, and the cooked, drained mushrooms. Add to cooked sauce and pour into a greased 1½-quart casserole. Top with remaining dried sprouts and bake in a 350°F. oven 25 to 30 minutes. Serves 6.

SOUTHERN SPROUT PIE

1½ cups dried sprouts

1 9-inch unbaked pie shell

3 eggs

1 tablespoon butter or margarine, melted

1 cup dark corn syrup

½ teaspoon vanilla

1 cup granulated sugar

1 tablespoon all-purpose flour

Spread dried sprouts over bottom of unbaked pie shell. In a bowl, beat eggs with an egg beater until foamy. Add butter or margarine, corn syrup, and vanilla. Beat until well blended. Combine sugar and flour and add to egg mixture. Beat well again. Pour over sprouts in pie shell. Let stand 10 to 15 minutes, until sprouts rise to surface. Bake in 350°F. oven 45 minutes. Sprouts will glaze during baking. Makes one 9-inch pie.

SQUASH (Summer Varieties)

Pick summer squash while they are still immature, before seeds form inside. Wash and cut in ⅛-inch slices without peeling.

Dehydrator: Spread slices over trays without overlapping. Dry at 120°F. 6 to 8 hours, until crisp, turning once.

Sun: Spread slices over trays without overlapping. Dry in full sun 8 to 10 hours, turning once.

Oven or Homemade Dryer: Spread slices over trays. Dry in oven or homemade dryer set at 120°F. until crisp, about 6 to 8 hours.

To Use: Slices are best eaten in the dried state. Eat with the fingers, as a snack, as a chip with dips or chop and add to salads.

Winter Varieties

Any variety of winter squash can be dried with excellent results. Cut whole squash in half and remove seeds and stem. Bake halves in 350°F. oven until tender, about 1-1½ hours. Scrape out pulp and mash.

Or cut squash in half and remove seeds and stem. Cut halves in thin slices and peel each slice. Cut slices into small cubes or thin strips. Cook in a small amount of boiling water, 35 to 45 minutes, in a steamer 45 to 60 minutes, or in a pressure cooker at 15 pounds pressure 12 to 13 minutes. Drain well.

Dehydrator: Line trays with plastic wrap and spread mashed squash over the wrap in a thin layer. Dry at 120°F. until squash can be pulled away from the plastic easily. Turn over and peel off plastic and dry other side until dried through, 8 to 12 hours. Break into pieces and process to a powder in a blender.

Place cubes and slices of cooked squash directly on trays and dry at 120°F. until pieces are crisp and hard, 8 to 12 hours.

Sun: Spread mashed cooked squash over plastic–covered trays and place in full sun in a well-ventilated area. Dry until top is hard and squash will pull away from the wrap easily. Turn over and pull off plastic. Continue drying until hard enough to break into pieces. Process to a powder in the blender. Drying will take 1 to 2 days.

Or spread cubes or slices of cooked squash in a thin layer over drying trays and place in full sun with good air circulation. Dry 1 to 2 days, stirring pieces occasionally and taking trays inside at night. Dried cubes should be hard and slices crisp.

Oven or Homemade Dryer: Cover trays with plastic wrap and spread cooked, mashed squash in a thin layer over wrap. Dry at 120°F. until squash is hard on top and can be pulled away from the plastic easily. Invert, pull off plastic, and continue drying on the other side. Dry 12 to 18 hours, until hard enough to break. Process to a powder in the blender.

Or spread cooked cubes or slices directly over drying trays and place in oven or homemade dryer warmed to 120°F. Dry 12 to 18 hours, stirring occasionally and rotating trays, until hard and dry through.

To Use: Pour 1 cup boiling water over 1 cup powder and let set 30 to 45 minutes. Use as you would cooked squash in casseroles and pies. Or add 1 cup boiling water to 1 cup dried cubes or slices and cook 30 minutes over low heat. One cup will yield about 1¼ cups cooked squash.

DRIED SQUASH-APPLESAUCE
SCALLOP

2 cups boiling water
1 cup dried squash
1 cup dried apples, chopped
¼ cup brown sugar, firmly packed
Few grains nutmeg
½ teaspoon salt
¼ cup butter or margarine, melted
½ cup evaporated milk
2 eggs, beaten
2 tablespoons butter or margarine
1 cup dried sprouts
1 cup dried bread crumbs

Pour boiling water over squash and apples. Cover and cook 35 to 40 minutes over low heat. Put into a blender jar. Add sugar, nutmeg, salt, ¼ cup butter or margarine, milk, and eggs. Process to a smooth puree. Pour into a greased, shallow baking dish. In a small pan, melt 2 tablespoons butter or margarine, stir in sprouts and bread crumbs, and blend. Arrange around edge of top of casserole. Bake in 350°F. oven 45 minutes. Serves 6.

GOURMET SQUASH

2 cups boiling water
2 cups dried squash, powdered
2 tablespoons butter or margarine

1 cup sour cream
¼ cup dried onions
Salt and pepper

Combine first 5 ingredients and season to taste with salt and pepper. Pour into an ungreased casserole and bake 30 to 45 minutes in a 350°F. oven. Makes 6 servings.

SWEET POTATOES

Cook unpeeled sweet potatoes until tender, 30 to 45 minutes in a 350°F. oven, 30 to 45 minutes in a steamer, or 8 minutes in a pressure pan at 15 pounds pressure. Peel and cut into ⅛-inch slices. Leave in slices or cut into sticks or small cubes.

Dehydrator: Spread slices, sticks or cubes of sweet potatoes in a single layer over trays. Dry at 120°F. until hard and brittle, 12 to 18 hours, stirring occasionally and rotating trays once or twice.

Sun: Spread slices, sticks or cubes thinly over trays. Dry 2 to 3 days in hot sun, until hard and brittle. Stir occasionally and take trays inside at night.

Oven or Homemade Dryer: Spread slices, sticks or cubes over trays. Dry at 120°F. 18 to 24 hours, turning occasionally and rotating trays once or twice.

To Use: Cook them in an equal amount of boiling water 35 to 40 minutes. One cup will yield about 1½ cups cooked sweet potatoes.

FRENCH FRIED
SWEET POTATO STICKS

1½ cups boiling water
1½ cups dried sweet potato sticks
1 egg, well beaten

½ cup dried bread crumbs
Deep oil, heated for frying

Pour boiling water over dried sweet potato sticks. Let soak 1 hour. Dip sticks in beaten egg, then coat in fine bread crumbs. Fry in deep hot oil until golden brown. Serves 4.

ORANGE-GLAZED
SWEET POTATOES

3 cups boiling water
3 cups dried sweet potato slices
⅔ cup sugar
1 tablespoon cornstarch
½ teaspoon salt

½ teaspoon dried orange peel, grated
1 cup orange juice
2 tablespoons butter or margarine

Pour boiling water over sweet potato slices in a saucepan. Cover and cook 35 to 40 minutes over low heat. Meanwhile, combine sugar, cornstarch, salt, and orange peel. Gradually add orange juice, stirring constantly. Cook over low heat until thickened. Add butter or margarine and boil 1 minute, stirring constantly. Pour over cooked sweet potatoes in a casserole. Cover and bake 1 hour, basting occasionally. Serves 4 to 6.

TOMATOES
(see also Green Tomatoes)

Peel tomatoes by dipping in boiling water 1 minute, then in cold water 1 minute. Slip off skins and cut out cores. Cut into ⅛-inch slices or in ¼-inch cubes. Drain well.

Dehydrator: Spread slices or cubes over trays so pieces are not overlapping. Dry 8 to 10 hours at 120°F., then turn slices and continue drying another 6 to 8 hours, until brittle.

Sun: Spread slices or cubes in a single layer over trays. Dry in hot sun with good circulation of air until tops are dry. Turn and dry other side. Will dry in 1 to 2 days in good weather. When drying is complete, pieces are brittle.

Oven or Homemade Dryer: Spread slices or cubes over trays. Dry at 120°F. until hard and crisp, 18 to 24 hours, turning slices and stirring pieces and rotating trays once or twice.

To Use: Refresh slices by placing on a shallow plate or platter and spraying with warm water. Let soak 1 hour, spraying with water occasionally. Refresh smaller pieces by soaking in water to cover an hour or more. Add dried slices or cubes without refreshing to salads, soups, and casseroles. One cup dried yields about 1½ cups refreshed tomatoes.

FRIED TOMATOES

1 cup boiling water	4 tablespoons butter or margarine
1½ cups dried tomato slices	1 cup milk
4 tablespoons all-purpose flour	Salt and pepper

Spray or pour boiling water over tomato slices spread over a plate or stacked in a water glass. Let soak 1 hour. Drain and coat refreshed slices with 2 tablespoons flour. Sauté in melted butter or margarine in a heavy skillet, cooking over low heat until lightly browned. Remove half the slices to a serving platter. Sprinkle the remaining slices in the skillet with the remaining flour and blend well. Gradually add milk and cook, stirring constantly, over low heat until thickened. Pour over tomatoes on platter. Salt and pepper to taste. Serves 4.

LAYERED DRIED TOMATOES

1 cup boiling water	2 tablespoons butter or margarine, melted
1½ cups dried tomato slices or cubes	1 cup dried bread crumbs
½ teaspoon salt	½ teaspoon dried oregano
⅛ teaspoon pepper	½ cup dried American cheese, grated

Spray or pour boiling water over dried tomatoes which are spread over a platter or stacked in a water glass. Let soak 1 hour or more. Drain and

138

arrange half the tomatoes in a 1-quart casserole. Combine salt and pepper, melted butter or margarine, bread crumbs, oregano, and grated dried cheese. Spread one-half this mixture over tomatoes in casserole. Top with remaining tomatoes and other half of crumb mixture. Bake in 350°F. oven 25 to 30 minutes until bubbling hot and lightly browned. Serves 4 to 6.

TOMATO PUREE

Core and cut up ripe tomatoes without peeling. Simmer 10 minutes, stirring occasionally to keep from sticking. Cool slightly and force cooked pulp through a food mill, colander, or Squeezo Strainer. In a shallow pan over low heat or in an electric skillet set at 260°F., cook juice down to a thick puree.

Dehydrator: Cover trays with plastic wrap and spread with an ⅛-inch layer of tomato puree. Dry at highest heat setting until firm and top is hard but sticky, 12 to 14 hours, and puree can be pulled away from plastic wrap. Turn over, remove plastic and discard. Dry another 12 to 14 hours, until hard and dry. Break into pieces and dry another 3 to 4 hours.

Sun: Spread a ⅛-inch layer of tomato puree over cookie sheets or drying trays which have been covered with plastic wrap. Dry in hot sun until hard and brittle, 2 to 4 days, turning once. Break into pieces and dry another 6 to 8 hours.

Oven or Homemade Dryer: Preheat oven to 150°F. Spread tomato puree in an ⅛-inch layer over trays lined with plastic wrap. Dry until firm, then turn over and peel off wrap. Dry another 12 to 14 hours, until hard and brittle. Break into pieces and dry another 3 to 4 hours.

To Make Tomato Powder: Pound pieces of dried tomato puree to a fine powder, using a pestle, a grater, or an electric blender.

To Use: For a tomato puree or paste, add ½ to ¾ cup powder to each cup boiling water. Stir well until dissolved and season to taste. For tomato juice, add 1 tablespoon tomato powder to each cup boiling water. Season with salt and serve hot or cold.

Or add 1 tablespoon powder to each cup liquid in soups, stews or sauces.

TURNIPS

Pull turnips after first hard frost or freeze. Wash, trim off top and root ends, and thinly peel. Cut into thin slices or chop into ¼-inch cubes. Dry without blanching for snacks. For cooking use, blanch 3 minutes in boiling water or 4 minutes in a steamer.

Dehydrator: Spread raw or blanched slices or cubes thinly over dehydrator trays. Dry 12 to 18 hours at 120°F. until hard and crisp. Stir once or twice and rotate trays once during drying.

Sun: Spread raw or blanched slices or cubes over drying trays in a thin layer. Dry in full sun where there is good circulation of air for 2 or 3 days, until hard and crisp. Stir occasionally and take trays inside at night.

Oven or Homemade Dryer: Spread raw or blanched slices or cubes in a thin layer over drying trays. Dry at 120°F. 18 to 24 hours, until crisp, stirring or turning occasionally and rotating trays once or twice.

To Use: Eat slices as a snack alone or with a cheese dip. Add chopped dried turnips to salads. Grind or process in blender and add to meat loaves and casseroles. Drop dried cubes in simmering soup stock for long, slow cooking. To cook as a vegetable, pour 1 cup boiling water over 1 cup dried turnips in a saucepan. Cover and simmer 35 to 40 minutes, until tender. One cup will yield about 1¼ cups cooked vegetable.

DRIED TURNIPS
IN A TOSSED SALAD

½ cup French dressing
½ cup dried turnip cubes

½ head lettuce
½ cup tomato, chopped

Pour French dressing over dried turnip cubes. Keep overnight in refrigerator. At serving time, tear lettuce in bite-size pieces. Add tomatoes, marinated turnips, and dressing. Toss until lettuce is coated. Serves 4.

SAUTÉED
DRIED TURNIPS

1½ cups boiling water

1½ cups dried turnip slices

½ cup flour

½ teaspoon salt

6 tablespoons butter or margarine, melted

Pour boiling water over dried turnip slices. Let soak 3 to 4 hours. Drain and dredge in flour which has been combined with salt. Brown in melted butter or margarine. Serves 6.

ZUCCHINI

Select slender, immature zucchini before seeds form inside. Wash, trim off ends, and cut into ⅛-inch slices. Blanching is not necessary.

Dehydrator: Spread raw slices thinly over trays. Dry at 120°F. until crisp, 12 to 18 hours. Turn slices and rotate trays once during drying time.

Sun: Spread slices thinly over trays and dry in hot sun with good air circulation. Dry until crisp, 1 to 2 days, turning slices occasionally and taking trays inside at night.

Oven or Homemade Dryer: Spread slices thinly over trays. Dry at 120°F. until crisp, 18 to 24 hours, turning and rotating trays once or twice.

To Use: Eat slices as a snack, alone or with a cheese dip. Use dry in salads or chop and sprinkle over the tops of casseroles. To fry, pour 1 cup boiling water over 1 cup zucchini slices and let set 3 to 4 hours. Drain, then dredge in flour and sauté in melted butter or margarine.

ITALIAN ZUCCHINI

2 cups boiling water
2 cups dried zucchini slices
1 medium onion, thinly sliced
2 tablespoons butter or margarine

1 cup fresh or canned tomatoes
Salt and pepper
¼ cup dried cheese, grated

Pour boiling water over dried zucchini slices. Let soak 1 to 2 hours. Drain. Cook onion slices in butter or margarine until transparent. Add drained zucchini slices. Cook and stir 5 minutes. Add tomatoes and season to taste with salt and pepper. Pour into casserole and top with grated dried cheese. Bake in 350° F. oven 25 to 30 minutes, until lightly browned. Serves 4.

Drying Meats

Fishermen and hunters, take notice: Here's a time-honored method of preserving and storing that deer you shot, or those trout you caught.

A time-honored method? Of course. Indians were using it in this country centuries before our explorers set out to spread learning among the noble savages and wound up learning a thing or two themselves.

Spanish explorers were among the early discoverers of this method of saving a bit of today's meat for tomorrow's meal. As they pushed through Mexico, Central America and the southwest part of this country, they found Indians cutting meat into long strips and drying it in the wind and sun. The Indians called this "charqui" and pronounced it like the last name of boxer Jack Sharkey. As English

143

explorers moved in, they picked up that name for dried meat, and it gradually changed to "jerkey" or "jerked beef."

Most Indian tribes used some method of drying meat, refining the system used. One advancement was to pound the dried meat with a rock, pound it and pound it, and gradually mix into it fat, dried fruits and vegetables. The result was "pemmican." That dish and today's variations of it provided ideal food, concentrated and energy packed, for the trail, be it the Long Trail or the war trail.

Another variation was probably originated by some ill-treated squaw on a rainy, cool day when nothing was going right. The meat hanging in the sun was suddenly hanging in the rain, and she knew that meant spoilage. So she carried the long strips of meat into the tepee and hung them there. It was a day when the fire was smoking and the tepee ventilation system needed servicing. Result was a new dish, smoked jerky, with a finer flavor and possibly longer lasting powers.

Today's hunters and fishermen can use these same historic methods for preserving food, and if they take care in their work, the results will be more than edible, they will be eaten with relish.

Meats may be dried in much the same way vegetables and fruits are dried. However, there are a few more precautions to take when drying meats than when drying fruits and vegetables. Meat is made up of both lean and fat portions and, while the lean keeps well when dried, the fat portion will soon turn rancid. To avoid this, only the leanest meat should be dried, and all possible fat should be removed before drying.

Select only very fresh, lean beef, venison, poultry, lamb, and fish for long-term storage. Very lean dried meats may be stored a year or more. Most cuts of pork do not dry well because of the high fat content, but lean portions of ham may be dried and stored for several months.

With one exception, meats to be dried should be fully cooked, which makes drying an ideal way of preserving leftover roast turkey or pot roast. The exception to using cooked meat is jerky. An explanation on jerky follows the instructions for drying cooked meats.

BEEF AND VENISON

Select a tender roasting cut with as little fat as possible, and trim off any bits of fat. Steam, braise or simmer in a small amount of water until tender, about 2 hours, or cook in a pressure cooker 35 minutes. Remove from heat, drain and cool. Cut into ½-inch cubes, keeping them as uniform in size as possible for even drying.

Dehydrator: Spread cubes sparingly over trays. Dry at 140°F., stirring occasionally, for 6 hours. Reduce heat to 130°F. and continue drying until cubes are hard and dried through. Test for dryness by cooling a cube and trying to cut through the middle. Well-dried meat should be too hard to cut easily and should have no moisture in the middle.

Sun: Spread cooked cubes in a thin layer over trays and place in a well-ventilated place in full sun. Dry until hard, stirring occasionally. Drying time will depend on the weather and the moisture in the meat, but should be from 2 to 3 days. Take trays inside at night.

Oven or Homemade Dryer: Spread cooked cubes in a thin layer over trays. Dry at 140°F. for 6 hours, then stir cubes and rotate trays and reduce heat to 130°F. and continue drying until hard. Keep door of oven or dryer ajar.

To Use: Pour 1 cup boiling water over 1 cup meat cubes. Soak 3 to 4 hours, until water is absorbed. Use in any recipe calling for cooked meat. Or, pour boiling water over meat and simmer over low heat 45 to 50 minutes. Then use.

DRIED MEAT-VEGETABLE
STEW

3 cups boiling water	½ cup dried parsnip slices
1½ cups dried meat cubes	1 tablespoon dried chopped onion
⅓ cup dried carrot slices	¼ cup all-purpose flour
½ cup dried peas	¼ cup water
½ cup dried green beans	Salt and pepper
½ cup dried celery slices	

Pour boiling water over dried beef or venison in a large stewing kettle. Simmer 1 hour, until meat is tender. Add dried vegetables and simmer another 30 to 45 minutes. Blend flour and water in a cup. Gradually stir into cooked mixture and cook, stirring constantly, until gravy is thickened. Season to taste with salt and pepper. Serves 6 to 8.

HAM

Select very lean, well-cured ham. Trim off all fat. Because it is a cured meat, ham may be dried without cooking, but it is more tender if it is cooked before drying. Cut into uniform sized pieces about ¼-inch square or in very thin slices, then into pieces about 2 inches wide.

Dehydrator: Spread pieces or slices one layer deep over trays. Dry 4 hours at 140°F. Lower temperature to 130°F. and dry until pieces are hard and dry through. Stir pieces occasionally and rotate trays once or twice during drying.

Sun: Spread pieces in a thin layer over trays and place in a well-ventilated area in full sun. Dry until hard, stirring or turning pieces occasionally. Drying will take 2 or 3 days.

Oven or Homemade Dryer: Spread pieces in a single layer over trays. Dry at 140°F. until hard and dried through, stirring or turning pieces occasionally.

To Use: Pour 1 cup boiling water over 1 cup pieces in a saucepan. Cover and cook over low heat about 1 hour, until tender. Use in any cooked dish or casserole calling for cooked ham. Dried ham should be used within 3 months.

DRIED HAM IN RICE

½ cup dried ham pieces
1 quart boiling water
1 cup uncooked rice
2 tablespoons dried, grated carrot
2 tablespoons dried chopped celery
1 tablespoon butter or margarine

2 teaspoons chicken flavored broth granules or 2 chicken bouillon cubes
½ cup boiling water
1 teaspoon soy sauce
1 tablespoon chopped chives or dried green onion tops

Simmer dried ham in water 1 hour over low heat, until tender. Add water to make 3 cups. Bring to a boil, then add rice, dried carrot, dried celery, and butter or margarine. Bring again to a boil, lower heat, cover and cook 20 minutes without lifting lid. Dissolve chicken granules or bouillon cube in ½ cup boiling water. Stir in soy sauce and add to cooked rice mixture. Mix lightly, put in a serving dish and top with dried, chopped chives or dried green onion tops. Serves 6 to 8.

DRIED HAM
AND APPLE DUMPLINGS

½ cup dried ham pieces	1 teaspoon baking powder
2 quarts boiling water	¼ teaspoon salt
1 cup dried apple slices	1 egg
2 tablespoons brown sugar	2 tablespoons butter or margarine
1 cup all-purpose flour	½ cup milk (about)

Cover ham with water in a heavy kettle. Bring to a boil. Simmer 1 hour, until tender. Add dried apples and simmer another 30 to 45 minutes. Add sugar. Meanwhile, in a mixing bowl, sift together flour, baking powder, and salt. Add butter, egg, and enough milk to make a stiff batter. Drop batter by spoonfuls into simmering liquid in pot. Cover and steam 15 to 20 minutes. Serves 6 to 8.

POULTRY

Select very fresh chicken or turkey. Duck and goose meat is too fat for drying. Steam or simmer until tender. Cool. Remove skin and any fat. Cut meat into uniform-sized pieces ¼ to ½-inch square.

Dehydrator: Spread cooked cubes in a thin layer over trays. Dry at 140°F. 4 hours, then lower temperature to 130°F. and dry until cubes are hard and dry through to center. Stir occasionally and rotate trays once or twice.

Sun: Spread cooked cubes thinly over drying trays and place in a well-ventilated area in full sun. Dry until hard, stirring occasionally. Test for dryness by trying to cut with a knife. Well-dried poultry should be too hard to cut easily. Drying time will vary, but should take 2 to 3 days.

Oven or Homemade Dryer: Spread cooked cubes in a thin layer over trays. Dry at 140°F. for 6 hours, keeping door ajar, then stir cubes and rotate trays and reduce heat to 130°F. Continue drying until hard and dry through.

To Use: Pour 1 cup boiling water over 1 cup cubes in a saucepan. Cover and cook over low heat 45 to 50 minutes, until tender. Use in any cooked dish or casserole calling for cooked poultry.

DRIED CHICKEN-NOODLE
CASSEROLE

4 cups boiling water	2 chicken bouillon cubes or 2 teaspoons chicken bouillon granules
2 cups dried chicken cubes	
¼ cup dried celery slices	½ teaspoon salt
1 tablespoon dried onion, minced	2 tablespoons dried parsley flakes
2 cups dried noodles	

Pour boiling water over dried chicken cubes in a stewing kettle. Cover and simmer 45 to 50 minutes, until tender. Add dried celery, onion, and noodles and simmer another 30 minutes, or longer, until noodles are tender. Add bouillon and salt. Sprinkle parsley flakes over top. Serves 6.

LAMB

Select a lean roasting cut of young lamb. Trim off any fat. Steam until tender or cook in a pressure pan 20 minutes at 15 pounds pressure. Cool and cut into ½-inch cubes.

Dehydrator: Spread cooked cubes thinly over trays. Dry at 140°F. 4 to 6 hours. Stir well, rotate trays and reduce heat to 130°F. Continue drying until cubes are hard and dried through.

Sun: Spread cooked cubes thinly over trays and place in a well-ventilated area in full sun. Dry until hard and dry to center, 2 to 3 days, stirring occasionally.

Oven or Homemade Dryer: Spread cooked cubes in a thin layer over trays. Dry at 140°F. 4 to 6 hours, keeping door ajar, then stir cubes, rotate trays and reduce heat to 130°F. Continue drying until cubes are hard.

To Use: Pour 1 cup boiling water over 1 cup cubes in a saucepan and simmer 45 to 50 minutes, until tender. One cup cubes will yield about 1½ cups cooked meat.

HERBED DRIED LAMB

1½ cups dried lamb cubes	1 cup dried onion slices
½ teaspoon chopped dried garlic	1 cup dried celery slices
¼ cup dried onion, chopped	½ cup dried tomato slices
1 dried bay leaf	½ cup dried peas
½ teaspoon dried basil	½ cup white wine
½ teaspoon dried oregano	6 medium potatoes, cut in 1-inch cubes
¼ teaspoon dried rosemary	¼ cup cornstarch
6 peppercorns	¼ cup water
4 cups boiling water	Salt
1 cup dried carrots	

Combine dried lamb cubes, herbs and seasonings and water in a large pan. Cover and simmer over low heat 1 hour until lamb is tender. Add dried vegetables and cook 30 minutes longer. Add potatoes and wine and cook 20 minutes more, until potatoes are tender. Remove bay leaf and peppercorns. Combine cornstarch and ¼ cup water in a cup. Remove meat and vegetables to a serving dish with a slotted spoon. Add cornstarch and water to liquid in pan and cook, stirring constantly, until thickened. Season to taste with salt and pour over meat and vegetables. Serves 6.

FISH

Clean and scale fish. Soak 30 minutes in a solution of ¼ cup flake salt dissolved in 1 quart water. Drain, remove skin and cut meat into small, uniformly sized pieces.

Or clean and scale fish. Leave small fish whole; fillet large fish or cut crosswise into steaks. Steam fillets 10 minutes, whole fish and steaks 15 to 20 minutes, until flaky. Remove skins and cut meat into pieces or flake with a fork, keeping pieces uniform in size.

Dehydrator: Spread pieces of fish sparsely over trays. Dry at 140°F. 2 hours, stir pieces, rotate trays, and reduce heat to 130°F. Dry until hard. Do not dry fish with other foods.

Or leave fillets, steaks, or very small fish whole. Remove skins and dry at 140°F. for 4 to 6 hours. Reduce heat to 130°F., turn fish and rotate trays, and continue drying another 4 to 6 hours before testing for dryness.

Sun: Lay pieces of cooked fish over trays and place in a well-ventilated area in full sun. Dry 1 to 3 days, depending on size of pieces. Turn or stir pieces occasionally and take inside at night.

Oven or Homemade Dryer: Spread pieces over trays. Dry at 140°F. 4 to 6 hours. Turn pieces, rotate trays, and reduce heat to 130°F. Continue drying until dry to center. Do not dry fish with other foods.

To Use: Soak fish in boiling water to cover. If fish is salted, discard any remaining soaking water and add 1 cup fresh water for steaming. If not salted, use soaking water to steam fish 10 to 15 minutes. Use as you would cooked fish. One cup will yield about 1¼ cups cooked fish.

DRIED FISH-VEGETABLE PIE

2 cups boiling water
2 cups dried fish
4 tablespoons butter or margarine
6 tablespoons all-purpose flour
¼ teaspoon pepper
3 cups milk
½ cup dried peas

1 tablespoon dried onion, chopped
½ cup dried celery slices
½ cup dried carrot slices
1½ cups boiling water
Salt
3½ cups seasoned mashed potatoes

Pour boiling water over dried fish. Let soak 30 minutes. If fish was soaked in salt water before drying, drain off water and add fresh. If not, use soaking water to simmer fish until tender, 10 to 15 minutes. Meanwhile, melt butter or margarine in a small saucepan over low heat. Stir in flour and pepper and gradually add milk. Cook, stirring constantly, until thickened. Set aside. Cook dried vegetables in 1½ cups boiling water until tender, 30 to 35 minutes. Drain. Combine cooked fish, white sauce, and cooked vegetables in a 1½-quart casserole. Season to taste with salt and top with a border of mashed potatoes. Bake in a 350°F. oven 30 to 45 minutes, until lightly browned. Serves 6.

JERKY

There are more methods for making jerky than there are Indian tribes. The most simple—but hardly the safest—was to cut the meat into strips and hang them in the sun.

Oceanside tribes improved on this by soaking the strips in seawater before drying them. That idea is still used by those who soak the strips in brine before drying.

Another Indian method was to hang the strips over a slow-burning fire of hardwood, or even an aromatic wood. The strips weren't near enough to the fire to cook, but were near enough to hasten drying and to keep off flies and other troubles.

Another step forward was taken when pepper was pounded into the meat, adding flavor.

The next step was a logical one—to soak the meat in a marinade. We find this the best way to produce a jerky that is tasty as well as nourishing.

Don't consider jerky an all-purpose food. It is, of course, high in protein, but it lacks both fat and vitamin C. It's fine for a few meals on the trail, since it can be eaten cold, requiring vigorous chewing, or can be the basis for many a recipe for stew.

Delicious, nourishing jerky can be made inexpensively of strips of almost any lean meat marinated in soy or Worcestershire sauce, brushed with liquid smoke or sprinkled with garlic powder or seasoned salt. There are many ways to add flavor to jerky.

No matter how well you make jerky, consider its shelf life short. Keep it in plastic bags or glass jars, so it will not absorb moisture, and store the containers in a refrigerator or a cool, dark, dry place. Eat the jerky within six months.

BEEF JERKY

2 pounds very lean beef (chuck or round)
¼ cup Worcestershire sauce
¼ cup soy sauce
1 tablespoon tomato sauce

1 tablespoon vinegar
1 teaspoon sugar
¼ teaspoon dried garlic, chopped
¼ teaspoon dried onion, chopped
1 teaspoon salt

Trim off all traces of fat from meat. Freeze until firm and solid enough to slice easily. Cut across the grain into very thin (⅛-inch) slices, then cut slices into strips 1 to 1½ inches wide. Meanwhile, combine remaining ingredients in a blender or shaker jar. Pour over meat strips that have been arranged in rows in a shallow baking pan. Refrigerate overnight, then drain strips.

VENISON JERKY

4 pounds venison
1 cup barbecue sauce
2 tablespoons liquid smoke

1 teaspoon chili powder
1 tablespoon Worcestershire sauce
Few grains cayenne pepper

Freeze venison until firm and solid enough to slice easily. Cut into ⅛-inch slices with a sharp knife or slicer, then cut slices into strips 1½ inches wide. Meanwhile, blend remaining ingredients and pour over venison strips that have been arranged in rows in a shallow baking pan. Marinate overnight in refrigerator. Drain well.

Dehydrator: Cover trays with strips without overlapping. Dry 4 hours at 140°F. Turn strips and rotate trays. Dry another 6 to 8 hours. Well-dried jerky should be dark and fibrous looking and brittle enough to splinter when bent in two.

Sun: Drying meat or venison jerky is not recommended in most climates.

Oven or Homemade Dryer: Lay strips of marinated meat in rows over trays, being careful not to overlap strips. Dry at 140°F. until strips will splinter on the edges when bent in two, 18 to 24 hours.

HAMBURGER JERKY

1 pound very lean ground beef	1 tablespoon Worcestershire sauce
1 teaspoon seasoned salt	¼ teaspoon dried onion, minced

For the leanest ground beef which will keep well in storage, buy ground beef with as little fat as possible or select a lean chuck roast and have it ground. Combine meat with other ingredients, mixing well. Cut a piece of plastic wrap the size of your drying tray. Put seasoned ground beef on plastic wrap and, using a moistened rolling pin, roll ground beef to ⅛-inch thick, spreading meat over entire area of tray.

Dehydrator: Place meat-covered plastic wrap on dehydrator tray and put in dehydrator set at 140°F. Dry 4 to 6 hours. Remove tray from dehydrator tray, plastic wrap–side up. Peel off wrap and discard. Return the top with a rolling pin to remove melted fat. Invert meat onto another dehydrator tray, plastic wrap-side up. Peel off wrap and discard. Return meat to dehydrator and dry another 4 to 6 hours. Top with paper toweling and roll again to absorb fat. Dry until jerky is hard and leathery. Cut into strips before storing.

Sun: Drying hamburger jerky is not recommended in most climates.

Oven or Homemade Dryer: Lay meat-covered plastic wrap on drying tray and place in oven or homemade dryer heated to 140°F. Dry 4 to 6 hours with door ajar. Remove tray to countertop and cover with a layer of paper toweling. Roll gently with a rolling pin to remove any melted fat. Invert meat onto another tray. Peel off plastic wrap and discard. Return it to oven or dryer for another 4 to 6 hours. Cover top with paper toweling and roll to remove fat again. Test for dryness before cutting into strips. Dried jerky should be hard and leathery.

CHEESE

Drying Dairy Products

Grate or shred any variety of cheese. Cheeses with high fat content will not keep long in storage, but may be refrigerated or frozen.

Dehydrator: Cover trays with paper toweling. Spread grated or shredded cheese over top. Dry at 120°F. until hard. Stir cheese occasionally and rotate trays and change paper toweling at least once as the melted fat accumulates. Drying will take 6 to 8 hours.

Sun: Cover drying trays with paper towels and spread grated or

154

shredded cheese over the toweling. Dry in full sun in a well-ventilated place until hard and dry, stirring cheese occasionally and replacing paper toweling at least once. Will dry in 1 or 2 days.

Oven or Homemade Dryer: Cover drying trays with paper towels. Spread cheese over trays and place in an oven or homemade dryer warmed to 120°F. Stir occasionally, rotate trays once or twice, and replace paper toweling at least once. Dry for 6 to 8 hours.

To Use: Try in cheese sauces, over Italian meat sauce, or to top casseroles.

MILK

Drying milk is a time-consuming process and perhaps not as satisfactory as buying the inexpensive dry milk powders available in the supermarket. It also has a shorter storage life because any cream in the milk has a tendency to turn rancid. However, if you have a surplus of milk and would like to try it, here's how:

Remove as much cream as possible from the milk by skimming or running through a separator. Pour a thin (about ⅛-inch) layer of the skimmed milk over drying trays which have been lined with plastic wrap or aluminum foil.

Dehydrator, Oven or Homemade Dryer: Dry 36 to 48 hours at 120°F. until milk flakes. Powder by pounding with a pestle or running through an electric blender.

Sun: Drying milk is not recommended.

To Use: This powder is best used dry in baked or cooked foods. Add ⅓ cup powder to dry ingredients and ⅔ cup water in place of 1 cup milk called for in recipe. To make 1 cup liquid milk, measure ⅓ cup powder in a measuring cup and add water to fill. Combine in a blender or shaker. It is more difficult to dissolve than the instant dry milk granules sold today.

155

EGGS

Dry only very fresh eggs. Because of the fat in the yolks, the storage life of dried eggs is not long, but they will keep well 3 to 4 months and are very useful for camping trips and vacation cabins. If you have laying hens, drying also is a practical way of storing eggs during the heavy laying season for use in the winter.

Beat whole eggs well, using an egg beater, electric mixer or blender. Pour beaten eggs in a thin (⅛-inch) layer over drying trays which have been covered with plastic wrap or aluminum foil.

Dehydrator, Oven or Homemade Dryer: Dry 24 to 36 hours at 120°F. until firm and dry on top. Turn over and peel off plastic wrap or foil. Dry another 12 to 24 hours, until hard. Break into pieces and dry another 3 to 4 hours. Pound into a powder with a pestle or by running it through a blender.

Sun: Drying is not recommended.

To Use: Try in baked goods such as muffins, pancakes, and cookies or in egg dishes calling for beaten eggs (see Scrambled Egg Mix, Hiking and Camping section). For each egg needed, combine 1½ tablespoons egg powder with 1½ tablespoons water.

Drying Grains

Freshly harvested grains often must be dried before being stored in airtight containers. Grain dryers are used for crops grown for commercial use, but grains grown and stored for home use may be dried in small batches in the kitchen or outside the kitchen door.

Grains such as wheat, barley, oats, and rye are harvested when the stalks are dry and yellow, but before the seeds scatter. Corn is dried on the stalk as long as the weather allows.

Ideally, grains should have a moisture content of about 10 to 12 percent to prevent mold and spoilage during storage. If you have access to a commercial tester, this is easily ascertained. If you do not, it is possible to estimate moisture content. The smaller grains are dry

157

when they have a hard, crunchy texture and a pleasant nutty taste when chewed. Well-dried corn kernels have a shriveled appearance or a dimpled end, depending on the variety.

Unless the grain is harvested in very dry weather, it should be dried to some extent before storage.

Dehydrator: Cover dehydrator trays with a ½-inch layer of wheat, barley, rye, oats, or buckwheat which has been partially dried on the stalk. Dry at 115°F. for 12 to 18 hours or longer, stirring occasionally.

Sun: Dry small batches of wheat, barley, rye, oats, or buckwheat spread thinly on trays in full sun. Large batches may be spread out on sheets of plastic in the sun. Dry 1 to 2 days, taking inside at night and stirring occasionally. Grain dried in the sun should be placed in a 125°F. oven 1 to 2 hours or stored in the freezer 2 to 3 days to destroy any insect eggs deposited during drying.

Oven or Homemade Dryer: Spread small grains in a thin layer over drying trays. Dry at 115°F. for 18 to 24 hours, stirring occasionally.

CORN

Dehydrator: Spread shelled corn over dehydrator trays in a single layer. Dry at 115°F., stirring occasionally and rotating trays once or twice. Drying time will vary from 12 to 18 hours.

Sun: Spread corn kernels thinly over drying trays and dry in hot sun where there is good circulation of air. Take inside at night and stir once or twice a day. Drying time will vary from 2 to 3 days.

Oven or Homemade Dryer: Spread shelled corn in a thin layer over drying trays. Dry at 115°F., stirring occasionally and rotating trays, until kernels are hard and dry through, 18 to 24 hours.

To Use Grains: Grind in an electric grain mill or hand grinder. If grinder is adjustable, set it at medium coarse grind for corn, at fine grind for smaller grains. An electric blender may be used to grind small amounts. Grind only enough grain to be used at one time. Ground grains lose flavor and vitamins in storage and are likely to turn rancid. Grains dried at the temperatures recommended may be used for seed. One cup dried small grains yields about 1½ cups flour. One cup dried corn will yield about ¾ cup cornmeal.

BOSTON
BROWN BREAD

1 cup finely ground dried wheat	1½ teaspoons salt
1 cup finely ground dried rye	¾ cup molasses
1 cup medium ground dried corn	2 cups buttermilk
1½ teaspoons baking soda	

Combine dry ingredients. Add molasses and buttermilk. Fill a greased 2-quart mold two-thirds full and cover loosely with foil. Set mold on a rack in a large kettle. Pour boiling water around the outside, half way to the top of mold. Cover kettle tightly and steam over medium heat 3½ hours, keeping water boiling around the mold the entire time. Add boiling water as needed. Remove mold from water, take off foil and run a spatula around the inside of mold to loosen bread. Invert mold. Serve hot.

Drying Grain Products

BREAKFAST CEREALS

Homemade breakfast cereals are delicious and far more nutritious than many commercially made ready-to-eat cereals. Try these for whole-grain goodness:

WHOLE WHEAT FLAKES

2 cups finely ground dried wheat (about)
1 teaspoon ground cinnamon
1 teaspoon ground nutmeg

½ teaspoon salt
½ teaspoon baking soda
¼ cup warm water
½ cup molasses

Combine 1 cup ground wheat with spices and salt. Dissolve soda in water and stir quickly into molasses. Add the flour mixture, then enough of the ground wheat to make a very stiff dough. Roll very thin and cut into strips.

Dehydrator: Lay strips on dehydrator trays without overlapping. Dry at highest setting until crisp, 4 to 6 hours. Remove and cool. Crumble into small, flaky pieces. Spread over dehydrator trays again and dry at highest setting another 2 hours, until very crisp. Makes 10 servings.

Sun: Lay strips over drying trays and dry in full sun where there is good air circulation. Dry until crisp, 6 to 8 hours, turning once. Crumble into small pieces and spread over trays. Continue drying another 2 to 4 hours, stirring occasionally. Makes 10 servings.

Oven or Homemade Dryer: Lay strips on drying trays. Dry at 150°F. 4 to 6 hours with door ajar, until crisp. Remove from oven or dryer and crumble, then return to trays and dry another 2 to 4 hours, until very crisp. Makes 10 servings.

To Use: Store in an air-tight container or in several small containers. Serve with sugar and milk as a ready-to-eat cereal.

CARROT CEREAL

½ cup brown sugar, firmly packed
1 egg
1 cup cooked carrots, mashed and cooled
2 cups finely ground dried wheat

½ teaspoon salt
1½ teaspoons baking powder
¾ cup rolled oats, uncooked
1 teaspoon vanilla

Combine all ingredients. Beat well. Cover drying trays with plastic wrap and spread batter thinly over plastic.

Dehydrator: Place batter-covered plastic wrap on dehydrator tray and dry at highest setting 4 to 6 hours, until top is firm and batter can be peeled away from plastic easily. Invert onto another tray and peel off and discard plastic wrap. Continue drying batter until hard and crisp, another 6 to 8 hours. Cool and crumble, then spread back over dehydrator trays and dry until very crisp, 2 to 3 hours. Makes 10 servings.

Sun: Place plastic-covered trays spread with batter in full sun in a well-ventilated area. Dry 4 to 6 hours, until batter can be pulled away from the plastic. Invert onto another tray and peel off and discard plastic. Dry batter until hard, another 4 to 6 hours. Take inside overnight. In the morning, crumble and spread over trays to dry until very crisp, another 3 to 4 hours or more. Makes 10 servings.

Oven or Homemade Dryer: Place batter on plastic-covered trays. Dry at 150°F. 6 to 8 hours with the door ajar, until batter can be peeled away from plastic. Invert onto another tray, peel off plastic and discard. Return batter to oven or dryer and dry until hard, another 6 to 8 hours. Crumble and spread flakes over uncovered trays. Dry another 3 to 4 hours, until very crisp. Makes 10 servings.

GRANOLA CEREAL

3 cups uncooked rolled oats
½ cup ground, toasted soybeans
½ cup sunflower seeds
1 cup coarsely shredded coconut

½ teaspoon salt
½ cup honey
1 teaspoon vanilla

Combine oats, soybeans, sunflower seeds, coconut, and salt in a bowl. In a cup combine honey and vanilla. Drizzle honey over dry ingredients and mix well. Makes 10 servings.

Dehydrator: Cover fine mesh trays with a thin layer of granola. (Coarse mesh trays must first be covered with cheesecloth or plastic wrap, which will lengthen drying time.) Dry at highest dehydrator setting, stirring occasionally and rotating trays once. Dry until crisp, 6 to 8 hours.

Sun: Spread granola over cookie sheets and dry in full sun until crisp, 8 to 10 hours. Stir occasionally.

Oven or Homemade Dryer: Spread granola over trays (or cookie sheets if mesh is too large). Dry at 150°F. until crisp, stirring occasionally.

To Use: Store in small batches in tightly closed containers. The oil usually used in granola is omitted for better storage. Serve as a snack or as a ready-to-eat cereal with milk.

OAT CRISPS

2½ cups rolled oats   ½ teaspoon salt
½ cup honey   2 teaspoons baking powder
2 eggs   1 teaspoon vanilla

Put all ingredients in a blender jar. Blend, adding just enough water to make a thick batter.

Dehydrator: Spread batter thinly (about ⅛-inch thick) over plastic-lined trays. Dry at highest heat setting until firm and dry on top. Flip over and peel off plastic wrap. Discard wrap and dry another 3 to 4 hours, until crisp. Crumble with the hands and return to dehydrator. Dry another 3 to 4 hours, until very crisp.

Sun: Spread batter thinly over plastic-lined trays or cookie sheets. Dry in full sun until firm and dry on top. Flip over and dry another 5 to 6 hours, until dry through. Crumble fine and return to drying trays. Dry until crisp.

Oven or Homemade Dryer: Spread batter thinly over plastic-lined trays. Dry at 150°F. until firm and dry on top. Flip over and peel off plastic wrap. Dry another 3 to 4 hours, until crisp. Crumble and return to oven or dryer. Dry another 3 or 4 hours, until crisp.

162

COCONUT CRISPS

2 cups grated coconut	1¼ cup rolled oats
½ cup brown sugar	¼ teaspoon salt
1 egg	2 teaspoons baking powder
1½ cups whole wheat flour	1 teaspoon vanilla

Combine all ingredients well. Add 1 to 2 tablespoons water if dough is too stiff to work. Roll out very thin. Cut into 3-inch strips. Makes about 15 servings.

Dehydrator: Lay strips on trays without overlapping. Dry at highest setting until crisp, 4 to 6 hours. Remove and cool. Crumble with the hands and spread over dehydrator trays again. Dry at highest setting another 2 hours until crisp.

Sun: Lay strips over trays and dry in full sun until crisp, 6 to 8 hours, turning once. Crumble into small pieces and spread pieces over trays. Dry another 2 to 3 hours, stirring occasionally.

Oven or Homemade Dryer: Lay strips on trays. Dry at 120°F. for 4 to 6 hours with door ajar. Remove from oven or dryer and crumble, then return to trays and dry another 2 to 4 hours, until very crisp.

To Use: Eat as a snack or with milk or cream as a ready-to-eat breakfast cereal.

GROUND NUTS CEREAL

1 cup buttermilk
½ cup dark corn syrup
½ teaspoon salt
1 teaspoon vanilla
½ teaspoon maple flavoring

1 teaspoon baking soda
¼ cup hot water
3 cups whole wheat flour
1 cup nutmeats, chopped

Combine buttermilk and syrup. Add salt, flavorings, and soda dissolved in hot water. Mix well. Add flour and nutmeats. Mixture should resemble cake batter. Pour into 3 greased cake pans and bake 40 minutes in a 350°F. oven. Cool on rack 10 minutes. Remove from pans and wrap in a damp dish towel until cold. Cut into chunks and grind in a meat grinder, using a coarse blade.

Dehydrator: Cover trays with plastic wrap or aluminum foil. Spread crumbs over covered trays and dry at highest heat setting 6 to 8 hours, until crisp through.

Sun: Spread crumbs over trays covered with plastic or aluminum foil or on cookie sheets. Dry in full sun 8 to 10 hours or more, until crisp. Protect from insects or birds with cheesecloth.

Oven or Homemade Dryer: Spread crumbs over drying trays which have been covered with aluminum foil. Dry at 120°F. 6 to 8 hours, until crisp.

WHEAT GERM CEREAL

2 tablespoons honey
3 eggs, well beaten
1 teaspoon salt
1 teaspoon vanilla

2 cups wheat germ
1½ cups whole wheat flour
1 cup dried plums, chopped

Combine all ingredients and mix well. Spread thinly over greased jelly-roll pans and bake in a 300°F. oven 20 to 30 minutes, until lightly browned. Cool well, then run through a food grinder, using a coarse blade.

Dehydrator: Spread crumbs over trays covered with plastic wrap or aluminum foil. Dry at highest heat setting, stirring occasionally, until crisp.

Sun: Spread crumbs over trays covered with plastic or over cookie sheets. Cover with a layer of cheesecloth and dry in full sun until crisp, 8 to 10 hours or longer.

Oven or Homemade Dryer: Spread crumbs over trays covered with plastic wrap or aluminum foil. Dry at 120°F. 6 to 8 hours, until crisp.

CRACKERS

Crackers dried in a dehydrator, the sun, or a homemade dryer are not intended for long storage, although they may be kept for a few weeks if tightly sealed when stored. They may be recrisped in the dehydrator or oven, if necessary. These crackers are a healthful, lightweight form of bread to take on camping or backpacking trips. Here are two recipes to get you started.

SESAME-OAT
CRACKERS

3 cups rolled oats, uncooked

1 cup finely ground dried wheat flour

1 cup all-purpose flour

1 cup wheat germ

¾ cup honey

1 teaspoon salt

¾ cup vegetable oil

1 cup water

1 egg white, slightly beaten

Sesame seeds

Combine oats, flours, wheat germ, honey, and salt. Pour oil and water into a well in the center and stir until mixture forms a dough that leaves the sides of the bowl. Divide into 4 parts. Roll each part out to a thickness of ⅛-inch and cut into cracker-size squares. Sprinkle tops with sesame seeds. Makes 8 dozen crackers.

CHEDDAR CRACKERS

1 cup finely ground dried wheat flour

½ teaspoon salt

⅓ cup butter or margarine, room temperature

1½ cups sharp cheddar cheese, grated

½ cup walnuts, finely chopped

¼ cup onion, minced

Dash of cayenne pepper

Combine flour and salt. Cut in butter and cheese, using 2 knives or a pastry blender. Stir in nuts, onion, and cayenne. Press dough into a mold such as a clean waxed paper box or plastic container. Chill in the refrigerator or freezer 3 to 4 hours. Slice thinly into ¼-inch wafers. Makes 4 dozen crackers.

Dehydrator: Spread crackers over trays in a single layer without overlapping. Dry at the highest dehydrator setting until tops are dry, 4 to 6 hours. Turn and dry another 4 to 6 hours, until crisp.

Sun: Spread crackers over trays without overlapping and place in full sun. Dry 6 to 8 hours, then turn and dry on the other side until crisp.

Oven or Homemade Dryer: Arrange crackers in a single layer over trays. Dry at 150°F. 4 to 6 hours, then turn and continue drying until crisp.

CORN CRISPS

1 teaspoon salt

2½ cups boiling water

½ cup yellow cornmeal

½ cup cold water

Add salt to boiling water over medium heat. Meanwhile, combine cornmeal and cold water in a small mixing bowl. Gradually add to boiling water, stirring constantly. Cook, still stirring, until thick. Cover and cook over very low heat 20 to 30 minutes, stirring occasionally.

Cover drying trays with plastic wrap. Drop a scant teaspoonful of cornmeal mixture on plastic wrap. Using the back of the spoon dipped in water, spread very thin. Continue over plastic wrap without overlapping crisps.

Dehydrator: Place plastic-covered trays in dehydrator set at 145°F. Dry until crisps will peel away from plastic wrap easily. Peel off, discarding plastic, and place them, inverted, directly on trays. Return to dehydrator and dry until crisp, another 4 to 6 hours.

Sun: Place plastic-covered trays in full sun. Dry 6 to 8 hours, until plastic can be peeled away. Place crisps directly on trays and dry another 6 to 8 hours, until crisp.

Oven or Homemade Dryer: Place on plastic-covered trays. Dry at 145°F. until firm, then peel off plastic sheet and place directly on trays, upside down. Dry another 4 to 6 hours, until crisp.

BREAD CRUMBS

Drying bread crumbs is a good way to make nutritious toppings for casseroles or coatings for meats from leftover biscuits or rolls and stale bread. Stale crackers also may be recycled in this way.

Dehydrator: Lay slices over trays. Dry at 145°F. 4 to 6 hours, until bread is dry enough to crumble. Grind through a food chopper, using a fine blade. Spread over trays again and dry another 2 hours, until crisp.

Sun: Lay slices over trays and dry in full sun 6 to 8 hours. Grind through the fine blade of a food chopper and return to trays to finish drying another 2 to 4 hours.

Oven or Homemade Dryer: Lay slices over trays. Dry at 145°F. with door ajar 4 to 6 hours. Crumble and grind in food chopper and spread crumbs back over drying trays and return to heat for another 2 to 4 hours.

CROUTONS

To make these delicious accompaniments for soups and salads, dice stale bread into small cubes and sprinkle with dried marjoram, onion salt, or garlic salt. If no fat is used in seasoning them, well-dried croutons will keep for several months tightly sealed.

Dehydrator: Spread thinly over trays and dry at 145°F. 4 to 6 hours, until crisp.

Sun: Spread in a thin layer over trays and place in full sun. Cover lightly with cheesecloth to protect from birds, if necessary. Dry 6 to 8 hours, until crisp, stirring occasionally.

Oven or Homemade Dryer: Spread over trays. Dry at 145°F. 4 to 6 hours, until crisp.

NOODLES

2 eggs
1 teaspoon salt

2 cups all-purpose flour
(about)

Beat eggs and salt with a fork. Gradually stir in as much flour as possible, then work in more flour by hand until dough is very stiff. Cut dough in half and roll out paper thin. Let set 10 minutes. Sprinkle with flour, roll up as a jelly roll and cut into thin crosswise slices. Repeat with other half of dough. Makes 3 cups noodles.

Dehydrator: Spread slices in a thin layer over trays and dry at 145°F. until crisp, stirring occasionally. Noodles will dry in 4 to 6 hours.

Sun: Spread slices thinly over trays and place in a well-ventilated area in full sun. Dry, stirring occasionally, until crisp, about 6 to 8 hours.

Oven or Homemade Dryer: Arrange slices in a thin layer over trays. Dry at 150°F. until crisp, stirring occasionally.

Drying Herbs

Herb leaves, seeds, flowers, and roots can add flavor and color to almost any food. Except for the seeds, whichever part of the plant is used, it is most flavorful and best for drying when young and tender. Pick leaves and flowers when flower buds are about half opened. If seeds are being harvested, they could be collected when the seed heads are turning brown—too early means the seeds have not ripened, too late means the seed crop may fall to the ground and be lost.

Pick before noon, as soon as the sun has dried off the dew. If you live in a dusty area, or know heavy rains have splattered your herbs with mud, try hosing them off the day before you harvest them.

169

Don't try to "pick" herbs as you might daisies. Cut them. Pruning shears are fine for this. Leave four inches of stem on leafy annuals. Cut only one-third the growth of leafy perennials. In both cases this permits further growth—and further harvesting.

The delicate flavors of herbs can be spoiled by heat and faded by sun. The flowers and green leaves or herbs should be dried at very low temperatures and away from direct sunlight. Good air circulation is important in order to dry herbs quickly and thus preserve their flavor.

Dry the leaves on the stems. It's easier to strip them off when dry than when green, and it's easier to dry them on the stem.

If a commercial dehydrator, oven, or homemade dryer is used, most herbs should be dried separately in order to keep their distinct flavors from blending. This precaution is not necessary, of course, with outdoor drying.

While the methods listed below are ideal for drying herbs, we would be remiss in our treatment of the subject if we didn't point out yet another method, one used for generations. That's to pick and tie small bunches of herbs, then to hang them in a room out of the sunlight. They'll be dry in about two or three weeks, and meantime will provide a decorative touch to the room.

An alternative to this is to tie the bunch in a brown paper bag, with the stem ends tied with the mouth of the bag, so the bunch hangs down inside. This reduces the light that reaches the herbs, cuts down on possible dust on them, and keeps errant leaves from falling to the floor. The bags should hang in an airy room.

Most herb leaves—the exception is bay leaves—are cooled and crumbled and stored in glass jars. Some, such as sage, oregano and marjoram, may be coarsely crumbled in the hands. The leaves of rosemary, savory, tarragon, and thyme may be crushed fine with a rolling pin.

Store large batches of herbs in several small glass jars. Small containers will retain the flavors better than large ones which lose aroma each time the jar is opened. To keep dried herbs at their best, always keep jars tightly covered in a dry, cool, dark place. If there is no dark storage area, jars may be kept in paper bags or in a covered can or box.

Do not store herbs in a cabinet near a stove, radiator, or refrigerator. The heat from them can cause loss of flavor.

Dried herbs are used in the dry state, without refreshing in water. The exception is rosemary, which should be added to the liquid of the dish and allowed to soak for a few minutes just before serving.

The flavor of dried herbs is much more pronounced than fresh herbs, so it is important to use very small amounts at first. To be safe, start with just a pinch. It is easy to add more, but the overpowering flavor of too much can spoil a carefully planned dish.

ANISE

Harvest anise seed when it begins to dry on the plant. No preparation is necessary.

Dehydrator: Remove alternate trays in the dehydrator. Spread seed stalks over remaining trays and dry at 110°F. until stalks and leaves are crisp. Remove seeds and dry through. Drying will take 10 to 12 hours in all.

Outdoors: Spread seed stalks over drying trays and stack in a well-ventilated shed or shady area. Or place each one upside down in a paper bag and hang in a shady, well-ventilated place. Drying will take several days, but they will need no attention during that time.

Oven or Homemade Dryer: Spread seed stalks sparsely over trays. Dry at 110°F. or less until stalks are brittle and seeds are dry through, 18 to 24 hours.

To Use: The licorice-flavored seeds are tasty in herb teas, sprinkled on sweet rolls or salads, and added to cookie batter before baking.

BASIL

Basil leaves must be dried quickly to prevent mold from forming. Snip stems of sweet basil as soon as they have developed in the spring. Discard any dirty leaves, but do not wash.

Dehydrator: Arrange herbs over dehydrator trays so they do not touch. Dry at no more than 110°F. until leaves are crisp enough to crumble in the hands, 8 to 12 hours. Cool, then crumble, discarding stems, and store.

Outdoors: Arrange leaves side by side on drying trays and place in a well-ventilated place out of direct sunlight. Dry until leaves are brittle enough to crumble, 1 to 2 days. Crumble, discarding stems, and store.

Oven or Homemade Dryer: Spread leaves in a thin layer over drying trays. Leaves will dry to brittle stage at 110°F. or less in 8 to 12 hours. Cool and crumble, discarding stems, before storing.

To Use: Add crumbled leaves to tomato dishes. Use to flavor soups, meat pies, and stews. Garnish peas, squash, and green beans with dried basil. Sprinkle leaves over lamb chops before broiling. Basil is especially good on fish, cheese, or egg dishes.

BAY LEAVES

Bay leaves are the shiny green leaves of the evergreen laurel tree which grows in warm climates. Pluck small mature leaves from the stems. Because bay leaves are one of the herb leaves that are not crumbled, the dried leaves should be handled carefully to keep them whole.

Dehydrator: Spread leaves over dehydrator trays and dry at no more than 110°F. until very brittle, about 6 to 8 hours. Cool and store whole.

Outdoors: Spread leaves over drying trays and place in a well-ventilated area out of direct sunlight. Dry, turning once, until leaves are very brittle, 10 to 12 hours. Store leaves whole.

Oven or Homemade Dryer: Spread leaves thinly over drying trays. Dry at 110°F. or less until crisp, 8 to 12 hours. Cool and store whole.

To Use: Add 2 or 3 dried leaves to soups, stews, and Italian spaghetti sauce. Cook 1 or 2 leaves with beef pot roast and baked fish. Add a leaf to the last water when boiling shrimp. Remove bay leaves before serving.

CELERY LEAVES

Remove leaves from celery stalks or accumulate them in a plastic bag in the refrigerator. Wash and drain dry. Chop or leave whole.

Dehydrator: Spread chopped or whole leaves thinly over trays. Dry at no more than 110°F. about 6 to 8 hours, until crisp. Crumble and store.

Outdoors: Spread chopped or whole leaves in a thin layer over trays and place in a well-ventilated shaded area. Dry 8 to 12 hours, until crisp. Crumble, discarding stems, and store.

Oven or Homemade Dryer: Spread chopped or whole leaves thinly over trays. Dry at 110°F. or less until crisp, 6 to 8 hours, with the door ajar.

To Use: Try dried leaves as you would celery, in soups, stews, salads, and cooked dishes.

CHERVIL

Pick small bunches of this herb in the spring when plants are immature.

Dehydrator: Dry whole bunches by removing alternate dehydrator shelves and arranging bunches thinly over trays. Dry at no more than 110°F., turning bunches once, until leaves are brittle, 12 to 18 hours. Cool. Chop or crumble leaves, discarding stems.

Outdoors: Tie stems with string and hang upside down in a well-ventilated, shady place until brittle. Drying will take several days.

Oven or Homemade Dryer: Arrange bunches over drying trays. Dry at no more than 110°F. for 12 to 18 hours, with door ajar.

To Use: Use 1 tablespoon to garnish salads. Add 2 or 3 tablespoons to flavor soups or egg and cheese dishes.

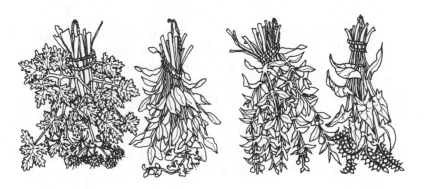

CHILI
PEPPERS

Red or yellow chilies may be mild or hot. There are several varieties. Dry whole or cut in half lengthwise or in thin slices. Separate mild and hot peppers or all the peppers will be hot.

Dehydrator: Spread whole, cut, or sliced chili peppers over trays and dry at 120°F. until hard and brittle, 12 to 18 hours. Stir once or twice and rotate trays during drying.

Sun: Spread whole, cut, or sliced chili peppers over drying trays. Dry in a well-ventilated area in full sun until hard and brittle, 1 or 2 days. Stir occasionally and take trays inside at night.

Oven or Homemade Dryer: Spread whole, cut, or sliced chili peppers over drying trays. Dry at 120°F. until hard and brittle, 18 to 24 hours.

To Use: Add 1 or 2 small, whole, or halved chili peppers—mild or hot— to each jar of dill pickles as they are canned. Drop 3 or 4 slices in soups, stews, and spaghetti sauce. Grind to use in chili powder (a recipe is included under Herb Mixtures). Use hot varieties carefully until you are accustomed to them.

CHIVES

Betty Jacobs, author of *Profitable Herb Growing at Home*, has advice on drying chives: Don't. She believes too much of the flavor is lost, and a pot of chives is easy to keep inside and productive all winter.

If you don't agree, try this: With scissors, cut chive tops from the plant before flowers form. Chop in ¼-inch pieces. Do not wash, but discard any dirty pieces.

Dehydrator: Spread chives in a thin layer over trays and dry at no more than 110°F. until brittle, 4 to 6 hours.

Outdoors: Spread chives in a thin layer over trays. Dry in a well-ventilated area out of sunlight 8 to 10 hours.

Oven or Homemade Dryer: Spread chives in a thin layer over trays. Dry at not more than 110°F. for 4 to 6 hours until crisp, keeping door ajar.

To Use: Dried chives add a mild onion flavor to salads and casseroles. Sprinkle 1 tablespoon dried chives over an omelet before cooking or into 2 eggs to be scrambled. Add 1 tablespoon with each cup of milk in a white sauce to add flavor and color.

CUMIN

Allow cumin seeds to dry as much as possible on the plant, but pluck pods before they burst and scatter seeds.

Dehydrator: Spread seeds over trays. If tray mesh is too large, cover with cheesecloth. Dry at 120° F. until seeds are hard and completely dry.

Sun: Spread seeds evenly over trays and place in a well-ventilated area in hot sun. Dry, stirring occasionally, until seeds are hard and dry, usually 1 day.

Oven or Homemade Dryer: Spread seeds over drying trays. Dry at 120° F. until seeds are hard, 6 to 8 hours.

To Use: Blend 1 teaspoon seed into 2 cups cheese or cheese spread. Add 1 teaspoon dried seed to each 2 cups liquid when baking bread. Grind it to add flavoring to sausage and game meats. Ground cumin is an ingredient of chili powder. A recipe for chili powder is included under Herb Mixtures.

DILL

Cut dill heads as soon as flower buds form but before all the buds are open. Chop, discarding stems. For milder flavor, snip off green sprigs and chop fine with scissors. Dill seed may be partially dried on the plant and gathered before pods burst and scatter seeds.

Dehydrator: Spread flowers or leaves or partially dried seeds over trays. Dry flowers and leaves 6 to 8 hours; seeds 4 to 6 hours at 120° F.

Outdoors: Flower heads or sprigs may be dried whole by hanging by the stem in an airy, shaded place. Dry under shelter 3 or 4 days, until crisp. Crumble and store.
Spread seeds over trays and place in hot sun. Dry 4 to 8 hours.

Oven or Homemade Dryer: Spread dill flowers or leaves over drying trays. Dry at 110° F. 6 to 8 hours, until crisp.
Spread seeds over trays and dry 4 to 6 hours at 120° F.

To Use: Add 1 tablespoon dill flowers or leaves to a dish of mashed potatoes or a pot of stew. Sprinkle 1 teaspoon over fish or apple pie. Stir ½ teaspooon into each cup of salad dressing. Sprinkle dill seeds over sauerkraut or cabbage. Add ¼ teaspoon or more dill seed to every quart of dill pickles. Use to garnish coleslaw and cooked vegetables. Make dill vinegar by steeping 1 teaspoon dill seeds in 1 pint of plain cider vinegar.

FENNEL

Pluck immature fennel leaves in morning after dew has dried off. Discard any dirty leaves, but do not wash. Fennel seed is harvested after it has dried somewhat in the pod but before the pods burst and scatter the seed.

Dehydrator: Spread leaves or seeds over trays. If tray mesh is too large, cover with a layer of cheesecloth. Dry leaves 6 to 8 hours at no more than 110° F.; seeds 4 to 8 hours at 120° F.

Outdoors: Spread leaves over trays and place in a well-ventilated, shaded area. Dry 8 to 10 hours, until crisp.
Spread seeds over drying trays which are covered with cheesecloth if necessary. Dry in full sun 6 to 8 hours, stirring occasionally.

Oven or Homemade Dryer: Spread leaves or seeds in an even layer over trays. Dry leaves 6 to 8 hours at no more than 110° F. and seeds 4 to 6 hours at 120° F., until leaves are crisp and seeds are dry through.

To Use: Add ½ teaspoon leaves to simmering soup and casseroles before cooking. Dried fennel seed adds a mild licorice flavor to candies, pastry, rolls, and cookies. Use ¼ teaspoon for each cup of batter.

FILÉ

Pick tender young leaves of the sassafras tree in the spring.

Dehydrator: Spread leaves thinly over trays. Dry at not more than 110° F. until leaves are crisp, 6 to 8 hours.

Outdoors: Spread leaves over trays and place in a well-ventilated, shady place. Dry 8 to 12 hours, until leaves are crisp.

Oven or Homemade Dryer: Spread leaves in a thin layer over drying trays. Dry at 110° F. until leaves are crisp, 8 to 12 hours.

To Use: Make a fine powder of dried sassafras leaves by processing in a blender or pounding with a pestle. Use filé powder as an ingredient in recipes for gumbo and other Creole dishes. Do not cook filé powder in the dishes, but add just before serving.

GARLIC

Peel and finely chop garlic bulbs. No other pretreatment is necessary.

Dehydrator: Spread chopped garlic over dehydrator trays. If mesh in trays is too large, cover with cheesecloth. Dry at 120° F. until crisp, 6 to 8 hours.

Outdoors: Spread chopped garlic in a thin layer over trays and place in a well-ventilated area out of direct sunlight. Dry 6 to 8 hours, until crisp.

Oven or Homemade Dryer: Spread chopped garlic thinly over trays. Dry at 120° F. for 6 to 8 hours, until garlic is crisp.

To Use: Store garlic as is or pound with a pestle or process in a blender to a fine powder. Add sparingly to salads or cook in Italian foods, omelets, and chili. Sprinkle over roast beef or add to salad dressings. Mix powdered garlic with salt to make garlic salt.

GREEN ONIONS

Pull green onions or scallions before the bulbs have developed fully. Separate the white bulbs from the green tops and chop tops fine with scissors. Using a knife, cut bulbs into thin slices.

Dehydrator: Spread green and white parts separately over trays. Dry green tops at not more than 110° F. 6 to 8 hours, until crisp. Dry white bulb slices at 120° F. 8 to 12 hours, until crisp. Stir occasionally.

Outdoors: Spread tops in a thin layer over drying trays and dry in a well-ventilated shady area until crisp, 8 to 10 hours.
Spread sliced white bulbs in sun until crisp, 8 to 12 hours.

Oven or Homemade Dryer: Spread tops thinly over trays. Dry 6 to 8 hours at not more than 110° F. until crisp.
Spread chopped green onion bulbs thinly over trays. Dry at 120° F. until crisp, 12 to 18 hours.

To Use: Add tops to salads, soups, and casseroles. Use bulbs as you would dried onions (see vegetables). Either may be pulverized to a powder and added to salt to make onion salt.

MARJORAM

Pick the gray-green leaves at maturity. Do not wash, but discard any soiled leaves. Do not pretreat.

Dehydrator: Spread leaves thinly over trays and dry at 110° F. until crisp enough to crumble in the hands, 6 to 8 hours.

Outdoors: Spread leaves in a thin layer over trays. Place in a well-ventilated area out of direct sunlight. Dry 8 to 12 hours, until crisp.

Oven or Homemade Dryer: Spread leaves thinly over trays. Dry at 110° F. until crisp, 6 to 8 hours.

To Use: Crumble leaves, discarding stems. Sprinkle over leg of lamb and beef before roasting. Use to season sausage and to add zest to stews and gravies. Sprinkle fine crumblings over hot lima beans, peas, and green beans.

MINT

Pick the leaves of peppermint or spearmint plants in early summer, when leaves are most fragrant.

Dehydrator: Spread leaves in a thin layer over trays and dry at not more than 110° F. until crisp, 6 to 8 hours.

Outdoors: Spread leaves thinly over trays and place in a well-ventilated, shady place. Dry until crisp, 8 to 12 hours.

Oven or Homemade Dryer: Spread leaves thinly over trays. Dry at 110° F. or less until crisp, 6 to 8 hours.

To Use: Cool, then crumble leaves, discarding stems. Use mint for making jelly, to add flavor to lemonade or for tea. Sprinkle crumbled leaves over roast lamb or cooked vegetables.

OREGANO

Pick oregano flowers and the outer leaves just as the flower begins to open. Dry quickly to preserve the flavor.

Dehydrator: Spread over trays in a thin layer. Dry at no more than 110° F. until crisp, 4 to 8 hours.

Outdoors: Spread in a layer over trays. Place in an area with good air circulation out of direct sunlight. Dry 8 to 12 hours, until crisp.

Oven or Homemade Dryer: Spread leaves and petals over trays. Dry at 110° F. or less until crisp, 6 to 8 hours.

To Use: Cool dried leaves and petals, then crumble fine before storing. Add 1 teaspoon crumbled leaves to tomato dishes, especially Italian dishes such as spaghetti sauce, pizza, and lasagna. Sprinkle ½ teaspoon over pork roast, beef stew, and omelets. Oregano is especially good with wild game.

PARSLEY

Cut parsley tops with scissors as soon as new leaves have formed. Parsley can be cut throughout the growing season. Dry whole sprigs or chop tops fine with scissors for quicker drying.

Dehydrator: Place sprigs or spread chopped parsley leaves over trays. Dry at not more than 110° F. until crisp. Sprigs will take 8 to 12 hours, chopped leaves will dry in 6 to 8 hours.

Outdoors: Spread chopped leaves over trays. Drying whole sprigs outdoors is not recommended. Place trays in a well-ventilated shady area. Dry until crisp, 8 to 12 hours.

Oven or Homemade Dryer: Spread tops over drying trays in a thin layer. Dry at 110° F. until crisp, 8 to 10 hours.

To Use: Just before serving, sprinkle flakes over soups, salads, and sauces. Add to dumpling batter and egg dishes. Use as a garnish for cooked vegetables.

ROSEMARY

Pick young, tender leaves of the rosemary plant as soon as their aroma has developed. Discard any that are soiled. Do not wash.

Dehydrator: Spread leaves in a thin layer over trays. Dry at no more than 110° F. until crisp, 6 to 8 hours.

Outdoors: Spread leaves thinly over trays and place in a well-ventilated area out of direct sunlight. Dry until crisp, 8 to 10 hours.

Oven or Homemade Dryer: Spread leaves in a thin layer over trays. Dry until crisp, 8 to 12 hours, at no more than 110° F.

To Use: Dried rosemary should not be cooked, but needs to soak a few minutes in liquid to revive its flavor. Add ½ teaspoon dried rosemary to the cooking liquid of potatoes, cauliflower, green beans, or peas a few minutes before cooking. Add ¼ teaspoon rosemary to ½ cup salad dressing or vinegar and let set a few minutes before tossing a salad. Rosemary is especially suited to lamb and lamb dishes.

SAGE

Pick gray-green sage leaves in mid-summer, when their flavor is fully developed. Discard any soiled leaves, but do not wash.

Dehydrator: Spread leaves in a thin layer over trays. Dry at no more than 110° F. until crisp, 8 to 12 hours.

Outdoors: Spread leaves thinly over trays. Dry in a well-ventilated shady area. Dry until crisp, 10 to 14 hours, stirring occasionally and taking trays inside at night, if necessary.

Oven or Homemade Dryer: Spread leaves thinly over trays. Dry at 110° F. 10 to 12 hours, until crisp.

To Use: Crumble leaves coarsely and discard any stems. Sage is a long-time favorite for sausage seasoning. Dried sage also adds flavor to cheese, poultry, omelets, and meat loaf. Sage dressing is a good accompaniment to pork.

SAVORY

Pluck the leaves of winter savory or summer savory as they develop full flavor. Young, tender leaves are best. Discard any soiled leaves, but do not wash.

Dehydrator: Spread leaves in a thin layer over trays. Preheat dehydrator to 110° F. and dry until leaves are brittle, 6 to 8 hours.

Outdoors: Spread savory leaves in a thin layer over trays and place in a shady area with good cross-ventilation. Dry until brittle, 8 to 12 hours.

Oven or Homemade Dryer: Spread savory leaves thinly over trays. Dry at 110° F. until crisp, 6 to 8 hours.

To Use: Cool, then crumble leaves, discarding any stems. Dried savory improves almost any bean dish. Add up to ½ teaspoon leaves for every cup of beans before cooking. Add ¼ teaspoon to bread dressings and sprinkle a small amount over pork roast or lamb before roasting.

TARRAGON

Cut the leaves and tops of young tarragon plants early in the day, as soon as the sun has dried the dew off the leaves.

Dehydrator: Spread leaves and tops over trays, removing every other tray. Dry at 110° F. until brittle, 6 to 8 hours.

Outdoors: Spread leaves thinly over drying trays and place in an airy, shady area. Let dry until crisp, stirring occasionally, 8 to 12 hours.

Oven or Homemade Dryer: Spread leaves in a thin layer over trays. Dry at 110° F. until crisp, 8 to 12 hours or overnight.

To Use: Cool dried leaves and tops, then crumble fine. Add a pinch of dried tarragon to tomato juice or to any dish made with tomatoes. A recipe for tarragon vinegar—a favorite dressing for salads— is included in this section.

THYME

Pick thyme leaves when plants first begin to flower. Discard any soiled leaves, but do not wash.

Dehydrator: Spread leaves in a thin layer over trays. Dry at 110° F. until leaves are crisp, 6 to 8 hours.

Outdoors: Spread leaves in a thin layer over trays and place in a well-ventilated area out of direct sunlight. Dry until leaves are crisp, 8 to 12 hours.

Oven or Homemade Dryer: Spread leaves thinly over drying trays. Dry at 110° F. until crisp, 6 to 8 hours or overnight.

To Use: Cool and crumble dried thyme leaves before storing. The strong, distinctive flavor of thyme adds character to meat loaf, onion soup or lamb in any form. Add a pinch to Italian dishes, stew, or wild game.

MICROWAVE
HERB DRYING

Researchers in the U.S. Department of Agriculture are experimenting with microwave drying, which heats and dries the food evenly throughout. Although this type of drying still is in the experimental stage, you may want to try it by drying a tray of herbs in this way:

Place a single layer of herb leaves between paper towels. Place the paper towels in a microwave oven and dry 1 to 2 minutes, depending on the thickness of the leaves. Cool and test for brittleness. Herb leaves are dry when they will crumble in the hands. If not dry, put back in the microwave and dry ½ to 1 minute longer.

HERB
MIXTURES

The flavors of some dried herbs are so compatible they have become traditional companions in certain dishes. The following are some of the favorite herb blends:

BOUQUET GARNI

2 sprigs or 6 tablespoons dried parsley

3 tablespoons dried celery leaves

3 tablespoons dried onion, chopped

1 sprig or 3 tablespoons dried thyme

Tie all herbs in a small piece of cheesecloth and immerse in a pot of simmering soup or stew. Remove and discard before serving.

184

CHILI POWDER

1 tablespoon dried mild chili peppers, chopped

¼ teaspoon dried hot chili peppers, chopped

1 teaspoon dried cumin seed

1 teaspoon dried oregano leaves

½ teaspoon dried garlic

1 teaspoon salt

Combine all herbs and pulverize to a coarse powder with a pestle or in a blender. Use for chili, barbecue sauce, bean dishes, or meat loaf.

FINES HERBES

(Fines Herbes is a French term for a combination of herbs used for specific dishes. They are finely chopped, mixed, and added to dishes just before serving.) The following are some Fines Herbes combinations:

FOR PORK DISHES

1 teaspoon dried sage

1 teaspoon dried basil

1 teaspoon dried savory

FOR BEEF DISHES

1 teaspoon dried rosemary

1 teaspoon dried parsley

¼ teaspoon dried garlic

FOR POULTRY DISHES

1 teaspoon dried sage

1 teaspoon dried savory

1 teaspoon dried parsley

FOR LAMB DISHES

1 teaspoon dried parsley   1 teaspoon dried marjoram
1 teaspoon dried rosemary

FOR FISH DISHES

1 teaspoon dried chervil   1 teaspoon dried savory
1 teaspoon dried parsley

FOR BEAN DISHES

1 teaspoon dried savory   1 teaspoon dried parsley
1 teaspoon dried onion

POULTRY SEASONING

This mixture of herbs is used in stuffings for veal and pork. It is a "must" for adding flavor to poultry.

1 tablespoon dried sage   1 tablespoon dried savory
1 tablespoon dried thyme   1 tablespoon dried rosemary
1 tablespoon dried marjoram

Add 1 or 2 teaspoons of mixture to any stuffing recipe.

Herb Teas

Teas made from the dried leaves of herbs can be soothing or invigorating, spicy or mellow, served hot or cold. It all depends on which herbs you select. Most herb teas are made by steeping the dried leaves in boiling water 5 minutes. The steeping should be timed carefully because too little steeping will leave the tea tasteless and tea that is steeped too long can be bitter.

CAMOMILE

Pick the daisy-like flower heads of the camomile plant as soon as they open fully.

Dehydrator: Spread heads in a single layer over trays. Dry at 110° F. until crisp, 4 to 6 hours.

Outdoors: Spread heads over trays and place in a well-ventilated, shady area. Dry until crisp, 6 to 8 hours.

Oven or Homemade Dryer: Spread heads in a thin layer over trays. Dry until crisp at 110° F. 8 to 12 hours.

To Use. In making tea, pour 1 quart boiling water over 1/3 cup heads and place in a warm teapot. Let steep 5 minutes. Strain. Drink hot or cold, plain, or sweetened with sugar or honey.

CATNIP

Pick young catnip leaves in early summer, before flower blossoms open.

Dehydrator: Spread leaves thinly over trays and dry at 110° F. until leaves are crisp enough to crumble, 6 to 8 hours.

Outdoors: Spread leaves in a thin layer over drying trays and dry in a well-ventilated, shady area. Dry until crisp enough to crumble, 8 to 10 hours.

Oven or Homemade Dryer: Spread leaves thinly over trays. Dry at 110° F. until crisp, 6 to 8 hours.

To Use: Crumble leaves and store in small glass jars. Place 1/3 cup leaves in a heated teapot. Cover with 1 quart boiling water and steep 5 minutes. Drink hot or cold, plain or sweetened.

COMFREY

Pluck the developing center leaves near the crown of the comfrey plant, discarding any that are overdeveloped or soiled.

Dehydrator: Spread leaves in a thin layer over trays. Dry at 110° F. 12 to 18 hours, or until crisp and completely dry.

Outdoors: Spread leaves thinly over trays and place in a well-ventilated, shady area. Dry until crisp enough to crumble, 2 to 3 days, taking inside at night and stirring occasionally. Crumble and store.

Oven or Homemade Dryer: Spread leaves thinly over trays. Dry at 110° F. 12 to 18 hours, until crisp. Crumble and store.

To Use: Place ¼ cup crumbled leaves and 1 tablespoon dried mint leaves in a pre-warmed teapot. Over this pour 1 quart boiling water. Let steep 5 minutes. Serve piping hot.

HOREHOUND

Cut a few woody branches of the horehound plant in midsummer, when plants are covered with bud clusters. Cut or break branches into 3-to 4-inch pieces.

Dehydrator: Spread pieces thinly over trays and dry 18 to 24 hours at 115° F. until dried through. Store whole branches in glass jars.

Outdoors: Spread broken branches over trays and place in a well-ventilated area in sun. Dry until branches snap easily in the hands, 2 to 3 days. Store whole pieces in glass jars.

188

Oven or Homemade Dryer: Spread broken pieces over drying trays. Dry at 115° F. 18 to 24 hours, until brittle. Store pieces in glass jars.

To Use: Break up three 4-inch pieces for each quart of water. Cover with cold water in a saucepan and slowly bring to a boil over low heat. Turn off heat and let steep 10 minutes. Dilute to taste. Serve hot, sweetened with honey.

LEMON BALM

Cut sprigs of the lemon balm plant when blossoms begin to form. Chop lemon-scented leaves and stems into ½-inch pieces.

Dehydrator: Spread chopped leaves and stems over trays in a thin layer. Dry at 110° F. until crisp, 6 to 8 hours. Crumble and store in glass jars.

Outdoors: Tie a few sprigs together with string at the stem end and hang upside down or spread chopped pieces over trays. Place in a shady area with good circulation and dry until crisp, 8 to 12 hours for chopped pieces, 2 to 3 days for sprigs. Store in glass jars.

Oven or Homemade Dryer: Spread chopped pieces over trays in a thin layer. Dry at 110° F. until crisp, 6 to 8 hours. Crumble and store in glass jars.

To Use: In a heated teapot, steep 1/3 cup leaves in 1 quart boiling water 5 minutes. Drink hot or cold, sweetened or plain.

LEMONGRASS

Cut long blades from the cactus-like lemongrass plant. Wash and drain well. With a pair of scissors, cut into ½-inch pieces.

Dehydrator: Spread blades thinly over trays. Dry at 110° F. until crisp enough to crumble in the hands, 6 to 8 hours. Cool and crumble before storing.

Outdoors: Spread blades in a thin layer over drying trays and place in a well-ventilated, shady area. Dry, stirring occasionally, until crisp, 8 to 10 hours. Crumble after cooling.

Oven or Homemade Dryer: Spread blades thinly over trays. Dry at 110° F. until crisp, 6 to 8 hours. Cool and crumble before storing in glass jars.

To Use: Measure 1/3 cup blades in a saucepan. Cover with 1 quart of cold water. Bring to a boil, turn off heat and let steep 10 to 15 minutes. Serve as a hot or cold beverage, plain or sweetened with honey or sugar.

PENNYROYAL

Pick pennyroyal leaves in the fall, discarding stems.

Dehydrator: Spread leaves over trays in a thin layer and dry at 110° F. until crisp, 6 to 8 hours. Cool and crumble before storing.

Outdoors: Spread leaves thinly over drying trays and place in a well-ventilated, shady place. Dry until crisp, 8 to 12 hours.

Oven or Homemade Dryer: Spread leaves over trays. Dry at 110° F. until crisp, 6 to 8 hours.

To Use: To make a delightful, mint-flavored tea, steep 1/3 cup dried pennyroyal leaves in 1 quart boiling water for 5 minutes. Serve piping hot with or without sugar.

ROSE HIPS

In late fall, after the leaves have dropped, cut partially dried, orange-red rose hips from rose bushes. Cut off and discard both ends and cut remainder into thin slices.

Dehydrator: Spread slices thinly over trays and dry at 110° F. stirring occasionally. Dry 12 to 18 hours, until crisp and hard.

Outdoors: Spread slices over trays in a thin layer and dry in a well-ventilated, shady area 2 or 3 days, until crisp and hard.

Oven or Homemade Dryer: Spread slices thinly over trays. Dry at 110° F. until crisp, 18 to 24 hours, stirring occasionally.

To Use: Although rose hips have little flavor, they are rich in Vitamin C and are a good winter source of that vitamin. Rose hip tea benefits from the addition of other herbs such as lemon balm or mint. To make rose hip tea, cover 1/3 cup dried rose hips with 1 quart cold water. Cover and slowly bring to a boil. Simmer over low heat 15 minutes. Strain liquid off, mashing the hips with a fork to extract all the vitamin-rich juice. Drink hot or cold with a spoonful of lemon juice and honey or sugar.

SASSAFRAS

Harvest the bark or root of the sassafras tree in early fall. Cut into thin shavings, chop fine or grind.

Dehydrator: Spread bark or root thinly over trays and dry at 115° F. for 8 to 12 hours. Cool and store.

Outdoors: Spread bark or root in a thin layer over trays and place in sun. Dry 1 to 2 days, taking inside at night and stirring occasionally. Cool and store.

Oven or Homemade Dryer: Spread bark or root thinly over trays. Dry at 115° F. 8 to 12 hours, until crisp. Cool and store.

To Use: Place 1/3 cup in a saucepan. Cover with 1 quart cold water. Place over low heat and slowly bring to a boil. Remove from heat and let set 10 minutes.

SOLAR TEA

Most herb teas may be made this energy-saving, vitamin-saving way. Just place ½ cup dried herbs in a 2-quart clear glass jar. Fill with cold water to within 1 inch of the top. Screw the lid on tightly and shake well. Place in sun for 5 to 6 hours. Strain off liquid and add sugar or honey. Chill before serving.

HERB
TEA BLENDS

For variety and delicious blending of flavors, try these combinations of dried herb leaves:

BLEND #1

2 tablespoons dried rose hip slices

3 tablespoons dried peppermint leaves, crumbled

2 tablespoons dried orange blossoms, crumbled

To Use: Simmer dried rose hips in 1½ quarts water for 15 minutes. Remove from heat. Add peppermint leaves and dried orange blossoms and let steep 5 minutes.

BLEND #2

2 tablespoons dried peppermint leaves

1 tablespoon dried rosemary leaves
1 tablespoon dried comfrey leaves

To Use: Steep in 1 quart of boiling water 5 minutes.

BLEND #3

2 tablespoons dried camomile flowers

2 tablespoons dried lemon balm leaves
2 tablespoons dried comfrey leaves

To Use: Steep 5 minutes in 1 quart boiling water.

COMMERCIAL TEAS

Add interest and flavor to commercial teas by adding ¼ teaspoon dried peppermint, spearmint, lemon balm, or thyme to a pot of steeping tea.

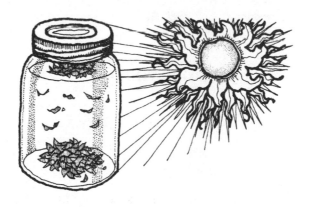

Herb Butters

Add 1 teaspoon dried dill, chives, chervil, fennel, marjoram, or tarragon to ½ cup butter or margarine. Blend well. Cover and leave at room temperature for 2 hours to blend flavors.

Herb butter may be stored for several days in the refrigerator. To use, spread over fried or broiled meat or fish. Just before serving, add to scrambled eggs or spread on bread when making sandwiches.

Herb Vinegars

Herb-flavored vinegars are an expensive delicacy in gourmet food shops. They add piquancy and zest to salads and cooked vegetables. Here are 4 recipes.

DRIED BASIL VINEGAR

1 quart red wine vinegar

1½ tablespoons dried basil leaves, crumbled

Bring vinegar to a boil. Remove from heat, add basil leaves and let stand 48 hours. Strain.

TARRAGON VINEGAR

1 quart red wine
1 pint cider vinegar
¼ teaspoon dried garlic

2 tablespoons dried tarragon leaves, crumbled
2 whole cloves

Combine ingredients in an enameled saucepan. Let stand 2 hours. Simmer 15 minutes over low heat. Strain and chill before using.

HERB WINE VINEGAR

1 quart white vinegar
1 quart dry red or white wine
1 teaspoon dried tarragon leaves, crumbled
4 whole cloves

2 teaspoons dried lemon balm leaves, crumbled
6 dried bay leaves
¼ teaspoon dried garlic, minced

Combine all ingredients in a kettle and place over low heat. Bring slowly to a boil, cover, and simmer 10 minutes. Strain through filter paper or a double thickness of cheesecloth. Cool. Store in tightly covered sterilized bottles. Makes 2 quarts.

SAGE VINEGAR

1 quart white wine vinegar

1 tablespoon dried sage leaves, crumbled

Heat vinegar to the boiling point. Turn off heat and add sage leaves. Let stand 24 hours before using. Strain.

Leathers

Leathers have almost as many names as they have uses. The first settlers in the Old West made leathers to preserve the goodness of fruits and vegetables that would otherwise have gone to waste. They called them "papers" because of their paper-thinness, or "fruit leathers" because of their pliable, leathery texture. Today they are often called fruit rolls or fruit taffy because of their delicious candy-like taste.

Leathers usually are rolled in waxed paper or plastic wrap and eaten (with relish!) with the hands. Children love them, and they're a wonderful substitute for candy. They also may be dissolved in water and used as a pie filling or as a dessert topping for ice cream or pudding, or to flavor yogurt.

Any fruit or vegetable or combination of them can be made into leather. They are an excellent way to use slightly overripe fruits. Almost-brown bananas have more banana flavor. Peaches that have ripened to the soft, juicy stage taste more "peachy." Both make better-tasting leathers than the just-ripe fruit.

Leathers may be made of raw or cooked fruits or vegetables, although the fresh flavor is preferred by many. Blend or stir the fruits and flavorings to a smooth puree, adding enough liquid (juice or water) to make the mixture thin enough to pour.

To make a puree, strain cooked or thoroughly ripened raw fruit through a food mill or Squeezo Strainer or liquify in an electric blender.

To convert this puree into leather, line a drying tray with a sheet of plastic wrap or brown wrapping paper. One dehydrator manufacturer offers a reusable Flexalon sheet for making fruit leathers, and others may be available.

Pour a small amount of the puree onto the plastic wrap or wrapping paper and tilt the tray until the puree is spread about 1/8-inch deep almost to the edges of the paper.

Use your imagination in making leathers. Try different fruits and vegetables, and different combinations, and vary the sweetening, seasoning and spicing to find what you like best. Remember, though, that fruits become more concentrated and therefore sweeter as they dry.

The times for drying will vary according to the amount of moisture in the puree and the depth of the layer you pour onto the trays. Drying should continue until leather is pliable but no longer sticky.

Dehydrator: Spread puree thinly in trays and dry at 120° F. 6 to 8 hours, until leather can be pulled easily from paper. Invert, pull off plastic or paper, and continue drying another 4 to 6 hours.

Sun: Spread puree thinly over covered trays or cookie sheets and place in a well-ventilated area in sun. Dry 1 day, or until leather pulls away from plastic easily. Invert and dry directly on tray or sheet 1 more day.

Oven or Homemade Dryer: Spread puree over covered trays. Dry at 120° F. 6 to 8 hours, until leather can be pulled away from paper. Invert onto another drying tray, peel off paper and continue drying another 6 to 8 hours.

To Store: For storing up to 6 weeks, roll up in waxed paper or plastic wrap, close and twist ends, and store in refrigerator. For longer storage, roll each strip in waxed paper or plastic wrap and seal in glass jars. Cut rolls to fit, if necessary. Leathers may also be stored flat separated by sheets of waxed paper, brown wrapping paper, or plastic wrap. Place layers in a cardboard box or metal box. Cover and seal with masking tape. Store jars or boxes in a dark, constantly cool place. Well-dried, well-protected leathers will keep a year or more.

RAW APPLE LEATHER

2 cups apples, peeled, cored, and cut into pieces

½ cup apple cider
¼ teaspoon ground cinnamon

Puree ingredients in a blender. Dry.

COOKED APPLE LEATHER

4 medium apples
½ cup water

¼ cup honey

Core and cut up apples without peeling. Add water and cook over medium heat 15 to 20 minutes, until tender. Force through a sieve or colander and stir in honey. Dry.

RAW APRICOT LEATHER

Immerse ripe apricots in boiling water 2 minutes, then in cold water. Slip off skins and cut in half. Remove seeds and drop into blender jar. Process until pureed. Dry.

COOKED APRICOT LEATHER

Cut apricots in half without peeling. Remove seeds. To every 2 cups of halves, add ½ cup water. Cover and cook over low heat until soft. Force through a sieve or colander, and dry.

BANANA LEATHER

Select ripe or overripe bananas. Mash well or puree. Spread on plastic or paper-covered trays and sprinkle with chopped pecans or walnuts and dry.

CHERRY LEATHER

2 cups tart cherries, pitted   ½ cup sugar

Combine cherries and sugar in blender. Process until sugar is dissolved and cherries are pureed, then dry.

RAW PEACH LEATHER

Select ripe or slightly overripe peaches. Peel and cut in halves, removing seeds. Puree in blender and dry.

COOKED PEACH LEATHER

Slice peaches without peeling and add ½ cup water and ½ cup sugar for every 2 cups sliced peaches. Cover and cook over low heat until peaches are soft. Force through sieve or colander and add ¼ teaspoon cinnamon or nutmeg. Stir well and dry.

PUMPKIN LEATHER

2 cups canned pumpkin or 2 cups fresh pumpkin, cooked and pureed
½ cup honey

¼ teaspoon cinnamon
⅛ teaspoon nutmeg
⅛ teaspoon powdered cloves

Blend ingredients well, and dry.

PINEAPPLE LEATHER

Cut whole pineapple into ½-inch slices. Core and peel each slice. Cut into pieces and shred or puree in blender, then dry.

PRUNE LEATHER

Soak 1 cup dried prunes overnight in 2 cups boiling water in a covered saucepan. Cook over low heat, without draining, 15 to 20 minutes, until prunes are tender. Force through a sieve or colander. Add ¼ cup lemon juice, stir well, and dry.

STRAWBERRY-RHUBARB
LEATHER

1 cup red rhubarb stalks, unpeeled, cut in 1-inch pieces	1 cup sliced strawberries
	1 cup sugar

Combine all ingredients in a covered saucepan. Stir well to dissolve sugar. Cook over low heat 10 to 15 minutes. Pour into blender and puree. Dry.

MIXED VEGETABLE
LEATHER

2 cups cored, cut up tomatoes	¼ cup chopped celery
1 small onion, chopped	Salt to taste

Cook over low heat in a covered saucepan 15 to 20 minutes. Puree or force through a sieve or colander, and cook in an electric skillet or shallow pan until thickened. Dry.

TOMATO LEATHER

Core ripe tomatoes and cut into quarters. Cook over low heat in a covered saucepan, 15 to 20 minutes. Puree or force through a sieve or colander and pour into electric frypan or shallow pan. Add salt to taste and cook over low heat until thickened. Dry.

Dried Soup Mixes

Dried vegetable mixtures are convenient for making soups at home or on camping trips. Their light weight makes them especially practical for hiking trips and they may be stored for long periods in vacation cottages.

Because of the differences in drying times of different vegetables, dried soup mixtures are made most easily by drying each ingredient separately and combining them. They should be stored in recipe-sized batches and kept sealed until used.

To use these dried soup mixes, add to boiling water and simmer 20 to 30 minutes, or until vegetables are tender. For a low-cost soup, simmer mixed dried vegetables in boiling water and flavor to taste with beef or chicken bouillon cubes or granules.

A delicious instant soup may be made from dried vegetables that have been powdered by forcing through a food grinder or processing with a blender. Add boiling water and cook a few minutes. Some vegetables that make excellent instant soups are tomatoes, peas, squash, spinach, carrots and almost any combination of favorite vegetables.

The following dried soup mixes are convenient for hiking and camping trips, and will save you time and money in the kitchen.

CREAMED PEA
SOUP MIX

2 cups dried green peas

½ cup dried onion, minced

½ cup dried celery slices

1 tablespoon dried parsley flakes

½ cup dry milk powder

½ teaspoon salt

⅛ teaspoon pepper

Combine all ingredients and store in a plastic bag, glass jar or any tightly covered container. To use, add to 3 quarts of water. Cover and simmer until peas are tender, 45 to 50 minutes. A ham bone or 3 or 4 bacon slices may be added, if desired. Serves 6 to 8.

MUSHROOM-BARLEY
SOUP MIX

½ cup dried barley

¼ cup dried mushroom slices

2 tablespoons dried onions, minced

¼ cup dried carrot slices

2 tablespoons dried parsley flakes

2 tablespoons dried dill

2 bay leaves

2 beef bouillon cubes or 2 teaspoons
  bouillon granules

Combine ingredients in a plastic bag, glass jar, or any tightly sealed container. Store in a dark, cool place. To use, add to 1 quart boiling water and simmer until barley is tender. Remove bay leaves before serving. Serves 4 to 6.

CREAM OF TOMATO
SOUP MIX

3 cups dried tomato slices
½ cup dried milk powder
1 tablespoon sugar

½ teaspoon salt
¼ teaspoon ground cinnamon

Powder tomato slices in a blender or with a pestle. Add remaining ingredients. To use, add to 1½ quarts boiling water and simmer 10 minutes. Add 1 teaspoon butter or margarine after cooking, if desired. Serves 4 to 6.

BEAN-PEA
SOUP MIX

½ cup dried pinto beans
½ cup dried navy beans
1 cup dried green beans
¼ cup dried celery slices
2 tablespoons dried onions, chopped

¼ cup dried carrot slices
4 whole peppercorns
¼ teaspoon dry mustard
½ teaspoon salt

Combine all ingredients and store in a tightly covered container. To use, add mixture to 2 quarts boiling water. Stir well. Boil 2 minutes. Turn off heat and let stand 1 hour. Cover and simmer 2 hours, until beans and peas are tender. Remove peppercorns before serving. Serves 6 to 8.

FISH CHOWDER MIX

2 cups dried fish, chopped
1 cup dried potatoes, chopped
½ cup dried carrots
½ cup dried onion, chopped

2 tablespoons all-purpose flour
½ cup dried milk powder
½ teaspoon salt
⅛ teaspoon pepper

Combine all ingredients. Store in a tightly covered container. To use, add to 1½ quarts boiling water. Stir well and simmer 30 to 40 minutes. Serves 6.

CAMPFIRE MINESTRONE

4 bouillon cubes or 4 teaspoons
bouillon granules

½ cup dried onion, chopped

½ teaspoon dried garlic, minced

½ cup dried navy beans

½ teaspoon dried oregano

2 bay leaves

6 peppercorns

1 cup dried tomatoes, sliced or
chopped

1 cup dried celery slices

1 cup dried carrot slices

2 cups dried green beans

2 tablespoons dried green pepper

1 teaspoon salt

Combine ingredients and store in tightly covered container. To use, add to 4 quarts boiling water and simmer over low heat 2 to 3 hours, until beans are tender. Remove bay leaves and peppercorns before serving. Serves 8 to 10.

TOMATO-NOODLE SOUP MIX

4 cups dried tomatoes

½ teaspoon salt

2 tablespoons dried onion, chopped

1 teaspoon sugar

½ cup dried noodles

Make a powder of dried tomatoes by pulverizing with a pestle or processing in a blender. Combine tomato powder with remaining ingredients and store in a tightly closed container. To use, add to 1½ quarts boiling water, stirring well. Simmer 20 to 30 minutes. Serves 6.

CREAM OF CELERY SOUP MIX

1½ cups dried celery slices

¼ cup dried onion, chopped

2 tablespoons all-purpose flour

½ teaspoon salt

½ cup dried milk powder

2 chicken bouillon cubes or 2 teaspoons chicken bouillon granules

Combine and store in a tightly covered container. To use, add to 1½ quarts boiling water. Cook over low heat, stirring constantly, until thickened. Cover and simmer 20 to 30 minutes longer. Serves 6.

205

CREAM OF MUSHROOM
SOUP MIX

1 cup dried mushrooms
½ teaspoon dried onion
½ teaspoon dried lemon rind, grated
3 tablespoons all-purpose flour

1 teaspoon salt
⅛ teaspoon pepper
1 cup dried milk powder

Combine all ingredients and store in a tightly covered container. To use, stir into 1½ quarts boiling water. Cook, stirring constantly until smooth and thickened. Cover and cook over very low heat 20 to 30 minutes. Serves 4 to 6.

VEGETABLE SOUP MIX

4 beef bouillon cubes or 4 teaspoons
    beef bouillon granules
½ cup dried carrot slices
¼ cup dried barley
¼ cup dried celery slices
½ cup dried green beans

¼ cup dried corn
½ cup dried green peas
½ cup dried tomatoes
1 bay leaf
6 peppercorns
1 teaspoon salt

Combine all ingredients and store in a tightly closed container. To use, stir into 2 quarts boiling water. Cover and simmer 30 to 40 minutes. Serves 6 to 8.

Drying
Flower Blossoms

Through the magic of drying, the fragrance of flower blossoms can be captured outdoors in summer, stored away in sealed containers and enjoyed indoors in winter.

Dried flower petals may be used in potpourri jars, sprinkled over lingerie in dresser drawers, crushed and added to bath water, or sewed into tiny cloth sachets and tucked between the sheets and towels in the linen closet. Wherever they are used, their fragrance will spread and linger in a delightful way.

Dry any fragrant blossoms available. Some of the best are roses—especially the wild varieties—apple blossoms, geraniums, lavender, marigolds, nasturtiums, and honeysuckle.

Dehydrator: Pluck the petals of just-opened flowers early in the day, as soon as the dew has been dried by the sun. Spread in a thin layer over dehydrator trays and dry at 110° F. until brittle, 6 to 8 hours.

Outdoors: Tie 3 or 4 flowers together with a string around the stem. Hang upside down in a well-ventilated, shady place until crisp, 3 to 4 days. Pluck petals from flowers.

Oven or Homemade Dryer: Pluck petals from flowers and spread thinly over drying trays. Dry at 110° F. 6 to 8 hours, or until brittle.

To Use Dried Blossoms: On a warm summer day, prepare dried blossoms in a potpourri—a combination of fragrances sealed in glass jars. Then some cold winter day, when the house is closed and stuffy and spring seems far away, open the jar for an hour or two and suddenly the room will be filled with instant summer. Or make several potpourri jars, enough so that you can keep one open all the time.

Make potpourri mixtures from any flowers, herbs, and spices available to you. The only expense necessary is for a small bottle of scent fixative which you can buy in most drugstores. Ask for gum benzoin or powdered orris root. Although it isn't absolutely necessary, the fixative retards evaporation of the oils which give the petals their fragrance.

Here are some recipes for potpourris. Once you get started, you'll be creating your own.

ROSE-GERANIUM POTPOURRI

2 quarts dried rose petals
1 quart dried geranium petals
1 cup dried peppermint leaves
½ cup lavender petals

8 whole cloves
1 tablespoon grated nutmeg
2 ounces gum benzoin or powdered orris root

LAVENDER POTPOURRI

3 quarts dried lavender blossoms
1 quart dried nasturtium petals
2 quarts dried rose petals

1 ounce gum benzoin or powdered orris root

GERANIUM POTPOURRI

2 quarts dried geranium leaves
2 cups dried geranium flower petals
1 cup dried spearmint leaves
1½ ounces gum benzoin or powdered
  orris root

1 tablespoon dried cardamom seeds,
  ground
1 tablespoon dried coriander seeds,
  ground

HERB POTPOURRI

1 quart dried sage leaves
1 quart dried rosemary leaves
2 cups dried thyme
1 cup dried oregano

1 cup dried basil
1½ ounces gum benzoin or powdered
  orris root

PINE POTPOURRI

2 quarts pine needles
1 quart dried juniper berries
1 cup dried sage leaves
1 cup dried parsley

2 tablespoons dried basil
1 ounce gum benzoin or powdered
  orris root

APPLE BLOSSOM POTPOURRI

2 quarts dried apple blossoms
1 quart dried honeysuckle blossoms
2 4-inch sticks cinnamon, broken
  into small pieces

2 cups dried rose petals
1 ounce gum benzoin or powdered
  orris root

To make potpourris, combine ingredients listed in a large roasting pan or mixing bowl. Toss gently, but thoroughly. Store in several tightly sealed glass jars, in a cool, dark place 5 or 6 weeks to allow the fragrance to develop.

To make sachets, sew the fragrant petals and petal mixtures inside small pieces of brightly colored material. Sachets usually are 2 to 3 inches square, but shapes and materials may vary from plain cotton to embroidered silks and needlepoint. Seal several sachets in a glass jar for a few weeks to blend aromas. Distribute them through closets and dresser drawers to lend their fragrance to stored clothes and linens.

Other Uses For Drying Equipment

Once it has become part of the household equipment, a commercial dehydrator or a homemade dryer can prove to be a very convenient appliance. You'll find their low, warm temperatures ideal for:

● Bread raising. Remove trays and preheat dehydrator or homemade dryer to 125° F. Turn off heat and place a shallow pan of hot water on the bottom shelf. Place covered bowl of bread dough on shelf directly above hot water. Let rise 1 hour, until doubled in bulk. Punch down and place in greased bread pans. Return to dehydrator until loaves are light. Bake.

● Making yogurt. Preheat dehydrator or homemade dryer to 110° F. Meanwhile, scald 1 quart of milk. Cool to 110° F. and add 1 tablespoon yogurt culture or ¼ cup yogurt containing live culture. Blend thoroughly. Divide into cups or containers and place on dehydrator shelves. Keep in dehydrator at 110° F. until set, 4 to 8 hours.

● Making cheese. The low temperature of a dehydrator is ideal for ripening milk to be made into cheese. To 1 gallon cooled, scalded milk add ½ cup buttermilk or yogurt, stir well, and place in a dehydrator preheated to 90° F. Let set 12 to 24 hours, until flavor has developed. Add 1 teaspoon liquid rennet or 1 rennet tablet dissolved in 1 teaspoon warm water and stir well. Let set 1 to 2 hours, until curdled. Cut the curd into small cubes and stir gently. Return to dehydrator and increase heat to 110° F. Hold at this temperature until curd is firm, about 30 to 45 minutes. Drain and press according to individual cheese recipe.

● Recrisping crackers and cereal. Crackers and cereal that have lost their crispness may be rejuvenated by spreading on drying trays and placing in the dehydrator or homemade dryer heated to 145° F. Dry 30 to 45 minutes, until crisp.

● Drying seeds. Seeds for the home garden may be dried without harm in a dehydrator if the temperature is kept at 100° F. or less.

● Curing nuts. Walnuts, hickory nuts, peanuts, and pecans may be cured in days instead of weeks by drying them at 110° F. in a dehydrator or homemade dryer.

● Decrystalizing honey. When a jar of honey crystalizes into a solid mass, as all honey eventually does, slip the jar into the dehydrator or dryer. Keep the heat at 110° F. a few hours and you'll have liquid honey again without any loss of nutrients or natural goodness.

● Drying crafts. Whether you're into ceramics, painting, or dough art, you'll find the dust-free warmth of a dehydrator ideal for drying craft work.

There are other uses for this convenient appliance. The more you use it, the more uses you'll find.

Index

Note: Pages in bold-face type indicate that instructions for drying are included.

213

216